HOMESTEADING WITH THE ELK

To Fran Bagley

My best wishes

A STORY OF FRONTIER LIFE IN JACKSON HOLE, WYOMING

From the author,

Bertha Chambers Gillette

By Bertha Chambers Gillette

Printed by
JACKSON PRINTING
Jackson, Wyoming

PREFACE and DEDICATION

This story is about the early pioneers of Jackson Hole, Wyoming. I dedicate it to my father, James Chambers, who at the time of the publication of this book, is 83 years old, and one of the surviving characters of that day. And to my sisters Margaret, Erma, and Dorothy; to my brothers Earl, Clifford, Jim and Lawrence, and to my most wonderful mother and brother Archie who have gone on to their places of glory.

A special thanks I wish to give to each person who gave his permission for me to use his name in this book, and to anyone who graciously gave me information which helped make this story possible.

Also, thanks to my husband, Wendell Gillette, who for weeks ate his meals at one end of the table, while the type-writer occupied the other, and who all the while kept urging me to go on with my story.

6 th

~~Fifth~~ Edition

CONTENTS

The Author
Bertha Chambers Gillette

Wedding Picture of
Berla Stevens and
James Chambers

James Chambers, age 25

Chapter 1
SIR HON

Daddy sat close to Pot Belly stove, rubbing some teeth on the leg of his overalls, then scraping the roots with his pocket knife. Mama sat opposite him on the other side of the stove with one foot propped up on a homemade stool close to the fire while she rocked Margaret's cradle with her other foot. She peered around the stove now and then to watch Daddy, but the sight of those bedraggled teeth with dried blood on the roots aggravated her nausea.

Old Timer, hanging on the kitchen wall, indicated the hour was approaching 10 p.m. Daddy and Mama talked of the cold, and neither of them could recollect any night in the land of the Tetons so cold or crisp as was that January 4th.

Mama squirmed on her chair, first on one hip then on the other, and occasionally bent over to rock the cradle with her hand. Her shins and feet were toasting while her back was freezing. She seemed more nervous than uncomfortable. She reached over to a drawer and took a brush from a pasteboard box and commenced brushing her long brown hair. As she brushed, sparks of electricity popped while her hair followed every stroke of the brush. When each lock had been smoothed, she took small bits of rags torn from an old white outing flannel petticoat, and wound small strands of her hair around the strips, then tied each rag close to her head.

Daddy laughed at her and said, "Babs, it's a good thing I didn't see you looking like this before I married you. You would scare a spirit away tonight."

Mama wasn't in the mood for a joke. "I couldn't have looked like I do tonight without being married." Then, with a tremor in her voice, she said, "There are only five more months left, and really I'm a little concerned."

"Concerned?" When there's five more months? Why

1

Babs, it will be summer by then and the roads will be good."

"But what about clothes? I need to be sewing, you know."

Mama spoke as if that thought had never stuck Daddy before. What she didn't know was that Daddy had spent many sleepless nights trying to figure out how to get a little money to clothe the expected baby.

Daddy quit polishing the elk teeth for a moment. He raised his eyebrows over the top of his forehead, pulling his eyes wide open, showing Mama his heart-felt affection. "Cheer up!" he said. "If it should come early, we will wrap it in one of those tanned elk hides I have tacked up on the shed."

At first Mama shuddered at the thought, but the more she pondered on it, the more she was convinced even an elk hide would be better than nothing on a cold night such as this.

Daddy dropped his eyebrows to a V-shape over the top of his nose and narrowed his eyes. "You may think of me as a worldly man, but I have a worried crust and a tender soul." He reached to the side pocket in the leg of his overalls and pulled out a file.

"I know! I've made a close study of manhood," Mama said. "You've been a man and given me cause to be proud. I guess it's just this cold creeping into my bones and stirring me up tonight." She shuddered and pulled the shawl closer around her shoulders.

"Now if you'll settle down, I'll tell you about the fight I saw today," Daddy said. "It was the worse fight I ever saw. Of course, I could have stopped it by shooting either elk, but somehow I didn't feel like a killer. Do you know what I mean? I just stood there behind two quaking aspens and let each one fend for himself.

"Around and around in the deep snow they traveled, first one direction, then the other. Several times I thought

2

they were bogged down in the snow so deep they would have to quit, but once Big Bull wallowed out, stabbed Little Bull across the rump with his antlers, and gored him in the ribs, till no animal on earth could take such punishment. They got up time and again to their hind feet, and tried to strike each other with their front hoofs. Finally Little Bull made a successful strike and lashed Big Bull across the front shoulder. He tore a gash wide open, and the blood spurted. This really made Big Bull mad.

"I tell you when bull elk get mad, they're really hostile. At first, I thought they were putting on a little show for my benefit, because the only time I had seen bulls fight this way was in the fall when the mating season was on; but a few seconds later I knew the bigger bull had his mind set on one thing, to be victorious: and he didn't care if I was there or not. I could tell the smaller bull wanted to quit several times. He knew he was fighting a ruthless battle, but Big Bull wouldn't let him. I don't know how long the fight had been going on before I saw it, but both looked plumb tuckered out. I followed their tracks through the trees. The snow was deep and crusted in places, but soft in others. If I didn't have snowshoes on I never could have followed them. I could see there had been a lot of stomping for a long way before they came to the spot where they decided to fight it out.

"About twenty minutes went by since I got there, and I got so cold standing in one spot I could hardly take it. I was about to leave when I heard a thud, crash, and a grind, and I could see they had locked horns. Little Bull was desperately pulling in one direction and Big Bull in the other until finally they fell to the ground. There was blood coming from the horns and nostrils, and froth from their mouths. All four eyes bunged in their sockets. Struggling to the bitter end and several minutes after Little Bull died, Big Bull let out his last cry with a gruesome, shrilly eeee call as if to say, 'I won! I lived longer than Little Bull.' He dropped one side

3

of his horns into the snow, and the other side of his and Little Bull's prongs stood skyward.

"I've heard that bull elk often lock their horns together like this and starve to death before they can free themselves, but these elk bled to death. I'll never forget that cry as long as I live. It echoed against the cliffs of the opposite canyon wall and bounced back.

"These two sets of teeth should bring me a little money. I can't see a crack in either pair, but by the time I get them polished, shipped off, and the money back, we'll be out of groceries and can use some cash."

Daddy got up and shoved another piece of pitchy pine into the heart of the fire. A black streak of smoke engulfed the room. Half choking, Mama said, "Sir Hon, one more puff of smoke that big, and we'll have to spring houseclean long before the dandelions show their heads."

"Now Babs," Daddy objected, "a piece of fire wood ain't no good unless it has some smoke in it. It shows it came from a good tar tree."

Sir Hon wasn't Daddy's real name, but one he grew up with. The name originated form the words Sir Honorable. Daddy acquired this name when he was in the fourth grade. He ciphered against all the other students in his room and won the contest; so his teacher presented him with a prize and said, "Sir, you are the honorable student this week."

All his classmates called him "Sir Hon" from then on. Mama used Sir Hon when she was stern with him and saved Jim as her pet name for times she wanted something special, such as his harnessing the team of horses and taking her into town to church. To some of his friends on Flat Creek, he was Sir Hon, and to others he was just Jim Chamber.

For a special nickname, Daddy called Mama Babs. No one else ever called her that. Her real name was Berla.

When Mama married Daddy, Grandma tried to discourage the match, because she worried about Mama's moving so far away into a country which had never been explored nor settled, but Mama, full of determination, had said to Grandma, "While I'm young, this sort of life will be exciting and when I get old, I'll be used to it."

Normally an uncomplaining soul, Mama right now was wondering what had ever possessed Daddy to take up squatter's rights up here in the wilds. She often spoke of the place as a wilderness and referred to Daddy's ranch as "Poverty Flat Creek Ranch."

Squatters rights gave a person the privilege of taking up a homestead if the land had not been surveyed previously; then he could mark off the land he wanted, put stakes up at each corner of the land, build a cabin on the homestead and live in it. If he lived there for five years, he could make his proof on the land and get a deed from the Government as soon as the land was surveyed.

Of course, Daddy didn't just squat there and let the grass grow up around him. Instead, he took his grubbing hoe and shovel and started building a canal. Mother Nature had already laid the blueprint for it. A tiny trickling stream wound itself down from Whistler's Peak, missed Flat Creek, and ran all by itself about nine miles before it emptied into Curtis's ditch. This little stream had helped Daddy decide where he wanted to build a home. He had chosen a spot right beside the stream so he could get a cool drink straight from the glaciers of Whistler's Peak any time of the year.

Daddy also knew with the Teton Range bordering him on the northwest, Gros Ventre Mountains on the northeast, Sheep Mountain on the southeast, and the Snake River on the southwest, he could have a good supply of water from glaciers, creeks, and tributaries all year around. He looked at the wide open spaces and the mountains ringing them and said, "Oh, the wonderments and miracles of creation! This is like love at first sight. Here is a new world and it's a good one. God must have had this little patch left over when He created the earth, so He surrounded it with these majestic mountains, put this beautiful stream here and called it 'Flat Creek.' Yes, this is really it. Nature doesn't often make places like this. These landmarks I'll call my friends. They will be here forever with their arms reaching out to help me."

He commenced building his cabin in this rugged, roadless, unspoiled land, surrounded by snow-capped peaks, with meager carpenter tools which consisted of an old rusty saw, a hammer, a butcher knife and an ax. In a few months, after much hard labor, he had erected a four-room cabin; two rooms on the ground floor and two unfinished rooms up above.

Something exciting happened inside Daddy's bosom when he stepped back, viewed his home through squinted eyelids, and thought, "This will be mine and hers."

Mama squirmed again on her chair and suggested they go to bed and save the kerosene for another day.

Daddy dropped the elk teeth into a pan of coffee and put them on the back of the kitchen range, hoping they would be a golden brown in the morning; then reached to the wall and took Old Timer from its hook and gave the winder several big turns.

"Maybe we had better sell the cow when the baby comes," Daddy said.

Mama looked as if she had seen that spirit Daddy had spoken about. "I'll never part with Old Boss. That cow is our very life," she said.

She got up to turn down the bed, when suddenly they heard a loud noise. Mama nearly fell over the foot stool and Daddy came close to dropping Old Timer.

At first, Mama thought of that bull elk fight; then she thought that the house was popping again as it did so often on cold nights. The logs would settle and pop, and sometimes the loud noise sounded like a rifle going off. Startled, Daddy and Mama stood staring et each other.

"What could that be?" Daddy asked. "It must be elk rubbing up against the house again. I saw a whole herd on the skyline tonight just at dusk."

They heard the noise again and recognized it as being a knock on the kitchen door.

They lived three miles from their nearest neighbor, and not even so much as a trail led from one house to another now. Drifts were high, making it almost impossible to get very far from one's own home.

Daddy took Carrie in his hands. Everything had to have a name so far as Mama was concerned; therefore she had named the kerosene lamp "Carrie." Daddy held it out in front of him so the reflection from it would shine on the face of whomever stood there. Wanting to have some kind of protection, Mama went for the butcher knife.

Opening the door, Daddy shook so hard the chimney nearly toppled form the lamp. There stood a huge man, his bulk filling the doorway. Daddy's eyes met him mid-drift because the man was standing on a snow bank. Daddy followed the large frame upward, but his head towered above the door.

"Hello Jim. Would you allow a questionable old man in your house this time of night?" He spoke with a strong voice, yet one of trustworthiness.

Daddy recognized the voice before he could see the face. He fairly screamed, "Why, Grandpa Knowlin!" Then he reached for Grandpa's hand to help steady him. "What on earth are you doing out in the cold this time of night?"

Mr. Knowlin, known to everyone on Flat Creek as being the finest, most sympathetic soul in the neighborhood, lived down in the swaps five miles from Daddy's place on the game refuge. His hands were so cold he couldn't untie the scarf, but Mama helped him get unwound. Daddy could feel

Grandpa trembling slightly while he tried to thaw the ice from around the buckles so as to free Grandpa, who still stood strapped to snowshoes.

"How in the world did you make it here tonight without perishing?" Daddy asked.

After Mama took his wraps, she put them over the back of a chair, and placed the chair close to Pot Belly. Daddy stood the snowshoes in the corner to drip dry.

"Whew!" Grandpa sighed, when finally free of all his heavy clothing. "I'm glad you and your Mrs. were still up. I'm not the kind that perishes, Jim. I'm the rough and rugged type that only the lightning can kill."

"I never cease to marvel at the ruggedness of you mountain men," Mama exclaimed as she pulled a chair close to the stove and offered it to Grandpa. As he sat down, he lifted his big, cold feet to the stool. His eyelids, folded with creases and drooping from age, half covered his magnetic eye, but the remaining sparkle reflected his power and enthusiasm.

For the first time, Mama noticed what a big man Dan Knowlin really was. She scrutinized him from the top of his head to his huge feet. He had little hair on his head except over the top of his ears and around the back. His ears stuck out larger than she had ever noticed; perhaps because they were red with cold. His hands were large and rough, partly because they matched the rest of his torso and partly because of the hard work and defying weather he had encountered.

"Yep, my life has been full of adventure—a little trip on snowshoes like tonight is needed exercise for me. I was born in Texas. I worked hard there and went to private schools. I married Laura Leonard in New Mexico, and she really has been wonderful and understanding. She didn't much like all this moving around while I was a Texas ranger, school superintendent, mineral surveyor, sheriff, a member of the Legislature and a game warden in Wyoming. I worked for a spell for the biological survey too, and investigated elk herds and antelope bands in Oregon, Washington, Idaho, Yellowstone Park, Alberta, Canada, South Dakota, and now Wyoming. But she hopes we are settled now down in the swamps. She loves it here and so do I."

Daddy and Mama knew Mr. Knowlin had not come this night to give them his life history, but that he had come on a special mission. Daddy and Mama exchanged wondering glances. All three of them were lonesome and were thrilled to get to talk with someone besides a shadow or an imaginary figure. They chatted awhile before Grandpa eventually came to his point. By this time, chewing his words excitedly, Grandpa sounded as if he were trying to spit out a whole mouthful of sentences at once.

"Jim, my boy, I'm planning on building a pole fence around every haystack on the elk refuge. We must keep the elk out of the stacks. How many poles would you reckon I will have to have?"

"How many stacks are you going to fence, and do you want buck fences, or are you going to drive posts?" Daddy took a pencil from the bib in his overalls and commenced scribbling.

"Sometimes we have sixty-seven stacks. I think a buck fence would be better if we could build it plenty tall, five or six poles high. Of course, posts around the stacks might be good enough. What do you think, Jim?"

"Buck fences are stronger all right." Daddy tilted his chair back and rocked on its two back legs.

"You see Jim, I've been hired to come here to act as refuge manager. First, Congress voted to purchase one thousand, seven hundred sixty acres of land from Robert Miller for forty five thousand dollars, then a year later they bought another thousand acres of public land. These elk have been wintering here instead of making that long migration trek to the Red Desert land south of Pinedale, where they had been going for years to get winter feed more easily."

"Yep," said Daddy. "The elk have lived and roamed here for years and years free of charge, but now they're finding large portions of the ancestral winter range occupied by ranchers and homesteaders. They are forced to raid hay stacks or die, and as it is turning out, they are doing a tremendous amount of both."

In a few minutes, Daddy figured out how many poles it would take.

"Now, Jim, the next question is—do you have any idea where I could hire a man to go to the timber for me and get the poles out? Eph Johnson and his twin brother, Jake, say they will trim them for me."

Mama's face turned the color of the inside of a watermelon on a hot summer day, all blushy and pink, as she saw Mr. Knowlin glance her way. She started figuring how many yards of outing flannel she could buy. She wondered if fifty yards would make all she needed. She even had visions of a little money left over for a frilly gown for herself for the special occasion. Daddy began mentally calculating how many hours he would have to spend alone in the timber, but knew he was man enough, with the help of his team, Old Dan and Bally, to haul the whole forest in before spring.

"Mr. Knowlin," Daddy said, trying to appear calm, "you are lookin' at the man who can do it. I'll be in the timber before sun-up in the morning."

"Now, my good friend," said Grandpa, "no use killin' yourself nor your horses the first day. I'm not that anxious for the poles. Take your time, my boy; take your time. If I don't get the fence up this year, I will next, or the next."

Try as hard as they could, they couldn't persuade Grandpa to stay over night. He had performed his mission. Knowing there was only one bed in the house, he felt Mama was in no condition to set up all night, nor to sleep on the floor while he occupied her bed. The only possible way for him to return to his home was the way he had come. He strapped his snowshoes on his feet, tied the warm, dry scarf around his face, pulled his cap down over his forehead, tucked his long gloves under his sleeves, and went humming off into the depth of the darkness.

"Know something, Babs?" Daddy asked. "I think he knows how badly I need that job. He has been a godsend to us tonight."

Mama admitted she had been praying silently every night for a long time.

The author and her daughter at the old homestead, years later.

Chapter II
SCAR FACE

Daddy beat Chanticleer up the next morning. In fact, he didn't even stop for breakfast. As he dressed, he put on an extra pair of drawers over his woolen underwear, buttoned his leggings over his trouser legs, put on a woolen plaid shirt, high-topped overshoes, a skull cap, then a red woolen cap with ear flaps over the top, slipped into a sheep-lined overcoat, and stuck an extra pair of gloves in his back pocket in case his mittens got wet.

He was well on his way when he heard Old Chan send his "good morning" crow. Chan had been hatched three years ago and was a wedding present to Mama from her father. The rooster of course took pride in being the first to awaken on the farm. What he didn't know was that Old Timer, from its hook on the wall, awakened first this morning.

Chanticleer did rule the roost and the barnyard too. He was a mighty fortunate rooster, as all the other chickens on the farm which had had the misfortune of hatching as males, had been put into a frying pan as soon as they were large enough. But because Chan had been a wedding gift to Mama, she kept him. Since he was such a pretty rooster, Mama felt his being around encouraged the hens to eat and sleep better.

Chanticleer wasn't afraid to tackle anyone or anything within his domain. Human, fowl or beast, it made no difference to Chan. Daddy carried either a club or a pitchfork with him when he crossed Chan's path, and every time Chan ruffled his feathers and scratched the earth in front of Daddy, he vowed if he ever got close enough to clobber the fowl, he would be chicken with noodles for the next meal. Mama was the only person who had him buffaloed. He must have known that part of the song which goes, "Don't bite the hand that's feeding you."

One time, Mama climbed a big snowdrift with a warm bucket of feed in one hand and a warm bucket of water in the other. She opened the door of the coop and was greeted by Chan, who let out a squawk as he sat in a nest filled with hay. She told Daddy she had never seen a funnier sight than Chanticleer sitting in that nest. Every time Mama entered the coop door, he would let out a screech and try to tell her something was wrong. After examining him, Mama discovered his feet and legs had been frozen and he couldn't bear to stand on the cold floor. His feet turned black and finally both of them dropped off. He hobbled around the rest of his life on two short stubs. This made Chanticleer a lot more humble and before he finally died, from old age, he was quite a mellow, yellow rooster.

Before Daddy had gone less than half a mile from home the horses were wallowing to their bellies in snow. Bally, being the taller horse, with longer legs, didn't sink as deep as did Dan. Talking in kind tones to his horses, Daddy coaxed them on through the drifts and biting cold. He did not feel to complain; even though at times it seemed almost impossible to reach his destination.

Great puffs of steam rolled from the nostrils of Dan and Bally, indicating a lot of mighty cold frost in the air. Before long, Daddy was beating his hands against his body, trying to keep the blood circulating. He removed the scarf from his neck and wound it around his face.

Cold as it was, the horses still perspired from work. After about five hours of hard labor for all three, with many rests in between, Daddy decided they had gone about as far as possible for that day. Taking his scoop shovel, he cleared away the snow, then gathered some dry pine boughs and built a fire. He led his horses close to it so they wouldn't catch cold while standing wet, to eat their bundle of hay which he had tied to the bob. Then he tried to eat the lunch

13

Mama had prepared in a hurry that morning while he was dressing, but finding it frozen, he put the bucket on the coals to thaw the sandwiches.

The sun was shining, but not one bit of warmth did it produce. Fortunately the wind didn't blow that day in the canyon. Using their same tracks, they descended the mountain and reached home just at dark.

Daddy fed his horses, watered and curried them, and then threw some fresh straw down from the stack for their bed. After saying to them, "No one would have to be a horse fancier to tell you are the greatest horse flesh in America," he told them how he appreciated what fine work they had done for him that day and promised them if they continued to do as well the next day, he would do all he could for them. From the way they rolled in the snow after the harnesses were off, Daddy could tell they were glad to be home again that night.

Standing by the kitchen range stirring supper, Mama greeted her husband with a smile. She spread a white tablecloth on the table, which was pulled over close to the stove. She opened the oven door so that Daddy could get the benefit of the hot oven while he ate his supper. She was a little disappointed at not seeing any poles on the sleigh, but thought maybe it was too dark to tell. "How many poles did you haul today, Sir Hon? she asked.

"Not a one, dear," Daddy replied. "Why it took me all day just to break a road. That snow was up to the horses' bellies in most places, and even to their backs in some. Perhaps tomorrow with good luck I might get a few trees felled." Mama thought this was slow business, even though sure he was doing the best any man cold do. She knew also that because Dan and Bally hadn't been worked very hard and were soft, Daddy had to use judgment as to how hard he dared work them.

The next morning, Daddy beat Chanticleer and Old

Timer both awake. He quietly crawled out of bed and shut the alarm off, so as to not awaken Mama. He planned to get his own breakfast this morning, but had never thought once about his lunch. Mama, hearing the lids of the stove rattle, got out of bed quietly, donned a robe, crept to the kitchen so as not to awaken Margaret, and had breakfast stirring before Daddy even had the fire going well. She prepared a big lunch and sent a bucket of milk with him to heat on the coals of his bonfire.

Soon he was off whistling. "There never was a man so lucky as I," he said to himself as the horses trotted off and were soon out of the sight of Mama, who stood at the window, peering out into the darkness. As she thought of the saying, "It is always the darkest just before dawn," she knew it would be another long, lonesome day.

After bathing and feeding the baby and putting her back to bed, Mama sat down with a mail order catalog, jotted down numbers, names, prices and postage. She figured the cost of all she needed. It came to twenty seven dollars and nineteen cents. Going over everything again, she cut out one package of safety pins. She thought of taking the yard of red calico off the list, but that was a must.

The mail order catalog was never destroyed—that is all at once. When it became outdated, it was taken to the little house out back where it served two purposes, one for sanitation and the other for meditation.

Laying the catalog down, Mama stepped to the door for more firewood. One thing Daddy always made sure of, and Mama could depend on, he had plenty of wood stacked against the back of the house, so all she had to do on cold, blizzardy days, was to step to the door and get wood for the fires without getting wet or cold. As she opened the door, a cold wave entered, so cold it looked like a fog rushing along the floor. Mama grabbed an armful of wood and hurriedly closed the door. She kept both fires going all day the one in

15

the kitchen, and the one in the bedroom. She knew it was useless to go to the window to look for Daddy, because the window faced West, and he had gone East, and it was too cold to open the kitchen door again to look, but that lonely feeling kept clawing at her heart, so automatically she went to the window. She parted the curtain to look out, but the frost, white and thick, had to be scraped off for a peek hole.

That night, Daddy came home again without any poles, but he did have a dead coyote. Coyote hides were selling for about ten dollars each if the pelt was a good one. This one was excellent. Daddy skinned it before he stopped for his supper. When he got the hide all stretched out on a board, wrong side out, he brought it in to show Mama how large it was.

"Oh, Jim dear," Mama explained, "you must have killed old Scar Face!" She was so excited she ran to her order blank to put the safety pins back on the list.

"No," said Daddy, "this isn't Scar Face, but I'm sure he has been filching the bait off one of my traps again. I saw his tracks in the snow, and they are much larger than this coyote's tracks. If I ever get old Scar Face, he will bring me double."

Mama had named this coyote Scar Face, for she and Daddy knew he was a great warrior. Many times, Daddy had found dead carcasses lying around where Scar Face's footprints were, and any animal who fights for food and a living, as Scar Face did, surely had scars on his face.

This king of the coyotes had been giving Daddy a good chase for two winters. Knowing the approximate location of his den, Daddy kept many traps set trying to catch him. Not only was Scar Face smart, but quick and powerful. One day Daddy found fur in his trap and Scar Face's tracks all around, and knew the coyote once more had jumped fast enough to remove the bait and miss the jaws of the trap so still roamed free. Daddy knew that Scar Face belonged to the wolf family and that he would fight for food when hungry.

"I'm taking old Meat-in-the pot with me tomorrow," Daddy said, and with these words got up from the table, took it from the gun rack on the wall, stood it in the corner and put some shells in his pockets. "I watched a poor, skinny, coyote hopefully examine the skeleton of an elk today which had already been picked clean by earlier scavengers. He was so thin his hair would be loose in his hide, so I'm glad he didn't get in one of my traps. One more day in the timber, I should have a load ready to bring out. I hope Grandpa Knowlin doesn't get impatient with me."

Mama didn't tell Daddy about the order. She knew it would be a long time before she could mail it, as the closest the mail sleigh came to them was one and a half miles away, and only Daddy and the team could get to the mail box when the drifts were high. Daddy had to pass the mail box on his way to Grandpa Knowlin's place and would pick up the mail then, but she still wouldn't have any money to mail with the order.

Daddy sat down, and using a whetstone, put a sharp edge on his pocketknife, wiped the blade across his overalls, and peeled an apple. He offered Mama a slice from it. She reached to take it, but remembering that that knife had just skinned a coyote, she declined as she shuddered at the thought of how close she had come to eating that piece of apple. "I shall never eat another apple Jim peels," she thought.

The next day was a hard day for Daddy. He had a good road to the timber now. The snow was trampled down enough so that he could at least manipulate his saw and ax. He felled six big trees and trimmed them that day. Wet from his hide out, he came home so stiff and sore that he could hardly unharness his horses. He didn't realize that he had big blisters on his hands until he took the reins to drive the

17

horses home. The palm of his right hand had formed one big blister and it had broken. The raw hide on his hand stuck to his wet gloves, but he didn't want Mama to worry so he came home whistling the same familiar tune he always whistled after dark. He whistled as a signal to Mama that he was coming. He practiced this habit ever since Mama had had a terrible experience when all alone with Margaret one night.

Having to leave home on business to be gone for two days and nights, Daddy asked Mama if she would like to go to one of her neighbors to stay rather than to stay at home by herself with the baby, but Mama hated to bother anyone, so decided to stay alone.

It was a night in October. When Daddy had kissed her goodbye that morning, the sun was shining, but by night a soft, feathery snow was falling. Mama decided to go to bed early and read until she got sleepy, so she put the baby in bed with her then opened her Bible to Psalms. The Bible was the only reading material she had besides the mail order catalog. Still reading by the light of Carrie, burning low, she noticed the lamp was nearly out of fuel. She looked at Old Timer which told her the hour was nine-thirty, so she decided to try to go to sleep. She put her Bible on a little stand close to her bed and blew out the light. Just as she did, she heard a noise and she thought it must be Daddy back so soon. "Is that you, Jim?" She called out, but no answer. Then she saw a shadow pass her bedroom window and she thought the cow or perhaps an elk had wandered near.

She heard the noise again. "Those pesky elk. I wish I had a good dog," she thought.

She got up, slipped her robe and slippers on and tiptoed to the door between the bedroom and the kitchen. From the crack in the door, she could see the kitchen window. There stood a man, as brazen as could be, trying to pry the window open.

Mama stiffened there in her tracks. She looked at Old Meat-in-the-pot on the wall, but had to cross in front of the window to reach it, and knew she was far too frightened to shoot.

She recalled putting a knife blade in each of the door frames, the one in the kitchen and the one in the bedroom, and remembered also putting a chair under the doorknob in the kitchen. Mama had no other way of locking her doors, but didn't know if this would hold an intruder out or not. She started to yell out loud, "Jim, someone must need help," but remembered she had already yelled, "Jim, is that you?" "Whomever this is knows my husband is away," she muttered.

Mama watched the man leave the window. He went to the kitchen and then she heard the knob turning. Her fright turned to anger, and she reached for Meat-in-the-pot. Mama knew how to shoot the gun as Daddy had made her do some target practicing just to get her familiar with how to handle the gun without danger to herself.

She worked the lever action to see if the gun was charged. Daddy never left a gun loaded. He hadn't this time either. Knowing he was short of ammunition, Mama looked into the box and found it empty, then remembered he had been coyote hunting the day before. Fighting her panic, she went to the cupboard drawer and got Big Butch, the knife used for heavy work like cutting up an elk or a hog. Mama tested it, and found it sharp and knew it would be a good weapon. She said, "I can use this on a man as well as an animal if I have to." Saying a prayer, she asked God to protect her.

Listening carefully, she couldn't tell if the noise she heard was that man tramping around the house or her own painful heart pulsating in her ears. Looking up at Old Timer on the wall, she glared desperately, trying to see what time it was, but the night being dark, she couldn't tell for sure what time the clock said, and knew this would be an all-night vigil, and perhaps the longest night she had ever spent. For about two hours, Mama traveled the inside of the house while the intruder circled the outside. Then she could hear him no longer. All was quiet, in fact, so quiet it frightened her. Even the wail of a coyote would have been welcomed at this moment.

Still too scared to go back to bed, Mama carefully placed a stick of wood on the fire as the house was getting cold. She put Copper-Topper, the tea kettle, on the heater, wrapped herself in a quilt, then sat by the fire. That log burned low, so she put another one in, then took Old Timer off the hook and carried it to the fire so as to tell the time of night from the light of the glow. It said two o'clock. Giving Old Timer another wind or two, she replaced it on its hook. Suddenly she heard another noise. This time the intruder was more brazen. "Oh, oh," Mama whispered, "he has been to the tool shed for some tools and he will surely try now to pry a door or window open."

Still having confidence in Big Butch, she held it tight in her hand. She heard Copper-Topper start to sing. "I will not only stab him, but I'll scald him," she murmured. Then she became aware that she wasn't nearly so frightened of his taking her life as she was of taking his, slumped in a chair again to catch her breath. "I will be the only witness to this crime, and oh dear, my babe may be born in jail." Offering another prayer, this time she asked God to spare her the agony of killing a man.

All at once, the intruder must have gone mad. He ran from door to window, from window to door, pounding on each one, but never uttering a word. Around the house he ran. Mama watched him pass the window in the kitchen then the one in the bedroom. She hoped he would soon wear himself out and drop from exhaustion, but he never did.

Just before daylight, he let out a yell that would have

20

turned sweet milk to clabber. Mama dropped to her knees and moaned. This was the last she remembered. When she revived, she crawled on her hands and knees to the kitchen window and could see daylight. All was silent and still. "This is the moment I've been waiting for," she exclaimed aloud in a weak, shrill voice, but it did not dissipate the terror that filled her.

The fire had gone out and Mama felt chilly, but didn't bother to rebuild the fire. She crawled to her bed, pulled herself upon it and wept. "What will tomorrow night bring?" she wondered.

When she awakened again, Margaret was fussing and demanded attention. Sitting on the front of the bed, Mama dangled her feet over the edge and still felt weak and trembly. She was thankful Daddy had carried in enough wood to last until he got home. Mama dressed, then went to the cellar underneath the kitchen to get enough fuel to fill the lamp once more. In order to get to the cellar, she had to unbolt the door and go down the steps into a dark hole in the ground. She was glad she didn't have to go outside. Daddy had made arrangements for Bill McInelly to milk Old Boss and feed her. Daddy told him to give the milk to the hogs, as Mama had enough to last her until he got home. She hadn't even heard Bill come nor go, and wondered if he had been there yet.

That night, Bill came back to milk the cow again. he came to the house and knocked on the door. Mama knew it was he, for she saw him coming. For the first time all day, she took the knife from the door casing, then invited him in.

"I was beginning to think maybe you had gone with Jim," he said. "Everything was so quiet around here this morning."

Mama didn't mention a thing about her experience the night before, nor why she had been so sound asleep she hadn't even heard him that morning.

When Daddy came home, Mama didn't have to tell him she had had company—someone, that is, besides Bill McInelly. He could see the tracks in the snow. He saw where a man had gone to the tool shed and while climbing over a partition in the wall had ripped his overshoe and stepped out of it, leaving it there. Daddy's tools were scattered, some were missing. Mama repeated her experience to him. It was like living that night all over again.

"Babs," he said as he held her in his arms, after investigating the scene, "I will put a strong lock on each door for your protection. And from now on, I shall always whistle when I get within hearing distance, so you will know it is I."

That was why Daddy again whistled this night as he came from the canyon. Mama opened the door and could dimly see the image of the horses approaching through the dark. She knew he was safe at home once more.

Chapter III
GREENBACKS

One night early in April, Daddy came home whistling a little louder, and a little more merrily than usual. He stopped his team close to the door, wrapped the lines around a pole which helped support his load. He leaped to the ground, took Mama in his arms, kissed her and said, "Berla, as soon as this load is delivered, we'll be sitting on easy street."

"I don't understand," said Mama. "Is this your last load?"

"Yep, my dear. Mr Knowlin will pay me tonight, then you can take the catalog out and order your clothes for the baby tomorrow."

Mama grinned and said, "Jim, you are the best husband a wife ever had. I'm so glad I married you, even if these last three months have been long and lonely for me."

"You know Berla," Daddy said, still holding her body close to his, "I think I'm buried here for good. When I first built this little cabin, I began to wonder, but our neighbors are so kind." Then pushing his cap to the back of his head, "I used to think when I left my home in Utah, I wanted a roving life, but guess now I'm here to stay 'till I pass the age of usefulness, and if you like it here, you can stay with me." He stooped a little and planted a kiss on her forehead.

That night when Daddy delivered his last load of logs, Grandpa Knowlin told Daddy he would be up tomorrow to settle with him, so Daddy asked him to have dinner with them. "Be there 'bout noon and Berla will spread a good table."

Mama primped extra prettily that next day, then asked Daddy to bring in some elk meat from the ice house. She pounded steaks, and they were so juicy and tender that when Grandpa Knowlin told Mama it was the best elk meat and corn bread he had ever eaten, Daddy looked over at her with

23

a gleam in his eye and said, "Isn't she a jewel?" Mama blushed, smoothed out her gathered apron to hide her broad-front form, and waddled along in slow gear.

While Mama washed the dishes, Daddy and Grandpa sat at the table talking about the snow roads breaking up so fast.

"It's a good thing you got through in the timber just when you did," said Grandpa. "The roads are getting too bare for a sleigh and too muddy for a wagon."

"Yep!" agreed Daddy. "An' every time I had to stay home because of blizzards, I worried for fear I couldn't keep my contract, an' several times I began to wonder if I was goin' to run out of poles. I'll tell you something now; there are few poles left in that forest.

"I'm mighty proud of how my horses fought through hunger and weariness. Sometimes sweat a rollin' from behind their ears and frost all over their bodies. They were tuckered out every night, but they knew as well as I they had to keep troddin' to meet the deadline before the roads gave 'way."

Grandpa had never asked Daddy what he was going to charge him, nor had Daddy ever asked what Grandpa would pay. They trusted and respected each other and that was all that mattered.

When Grandpa was ready to leave, he arose politely, thanked Mama for the delicious meal, and presented Daddy with a match box and said, "My dear boy, this is your pay for a job well done."

Daddy thanked him and said, "I'll feel good when I see that fence all up." He offered to take Grandpa home, but Grandpa declined, saying he needed the exercise.

After grandpa left, Daddy opened the match box and handed it to Mama. "Here Babs, you count it."

Mama unfolded the greenbacks and started counting. "Twenty, forty, sixty, seventy, five, eighty, five, ninety, one

24

hundred." She could see there were more bills left, and lots of them.

Daddy was so excited he reached for the box and started counting. "Two hundred, fifty, three hundred." That was more money than Daddy had ever earned in a year's time before. "Maybe we're not headed for the poorhouse after all."

Mama, feeling a little dizzy, took a corner of her apron and wiped a tear from her eye.

"Do you know what I'm going to do Berla?" Daddy asked while still clinching the match box. "I'm going to help Grandpa Knowlin build that fence and I won't let him pay me a dime. Bless his old charitable heart. That was a chunk of money. A better friend never lived. I will take old Dan and Bally and we will haul those poles to the mill."

The next day, Daddy just had to stay home to build the old sow a shelter. She was going to farrow before long, and Daddy was hoping for at least ten healthy piglets. Mama put on her wraps, bundled Margaret in blankets, and helped Daddy most of the day. He wouldn't let her do much, but she held slabs in place and handed him nails, and he was thankful for her company.

Daddy showed uneasiness all day. Mama sensed this early in the morning. "Jim, what is the matter with you?" she asked. It was about four o'clock.

Daddy tried to sound calm and answered, "I guess I just feel guilty not helping Grandpa Knowlin today."

"Well, dear, tonight you will be glad to know old Red has a clean, warm bed with a shelter over it where she can lay her tired body down for a rest. We females can sympathize with each other. Tomorrow you can help Grandpa Knowlin."

Daddy's only remark was, "You go get supper on while I put the sleigh box back on the runners."

Mama boiled rice for the main meal and served baking

25

powder biscuits with warm honey for choice dessert.

Daddy pulled his shoes off and said he thought he would retire early. Mama got the catalog, went over the order again and added: 36742—1—nightgown—size 36—blue. She wound Old Timer, blew out Carrie and carefully slipped into bed beside Daddy.

With the early dawn, Daddy stretched in bed, sighed a "ho, hum" and snatched himself back to consciousness, then let his arm fall across Mama's chest.

Not knowing whether this was intentional or not, Mama asked, "Are you wishing your misery might find company?"

"Nope," he answered, "just thought I'd get up an' shave an' shove off to help Grandpa Knowlin." He jerked himself out of bed with a flip and said, "No use gettin' yourself all woke up now, Berla. Stay there an' rest. I'll fry myself an egg an' be gone."

"Will you take that order I made out to Montgomery and mail it on your way? I left it on the table last night—and, oh, bring me back the mail," she said.

"Giddyup!" said Daddy, as he slapped the reins to Dan and Bally. The horses broke into a leisurely trot and jogged off down the one-track road. It was still crusted underneath this early in the morning, even though a soft, fluffy snow had fallen during the night and had added about six inches of new snow above the crust.

On arriving at the mail box, Daddy took the little bit of mail from it, then posted the order. He wound the reins loosely over the rein post at the front of the sleigh while he read a letter from Grandma.

Grandpa had other plans for the day; he usually did. Daddy should have learned a long time ago that Grandpa did just what he wanted to when the situation arose, acting on impulse or waiting for destiny; however, he took enough time to review the past with Daddy, but planned nothing for the future.

"Jim, I told you once before I'm not in a hurry to build that fence." He picked up a stick of wood and notched it with his pocket knife. "I'm a lot more anxious for Berla to have that baby. Go home and stay with her. I'll let you know when I'm ready to go to work."

As weeks and months went on, it was depressing to Daddy to watch the poles lie there and rot, but Grandpa wasn't depressed—they had already served the one-fold purpose he meant for them to serve.

Chapter IV
TIME FOR THE RED FLAG

On a Wednesday morning two months later, Daddy came in one day about noon wiping the sweat from his brow. His dark brown hair, matted to his head, looked slick and shiny. "Whew! It beats all how cold it can be one day, and hot the next. This is the funniest country I ever lived in. Its moods change so fast. It not only changes with seasons, but with the hour and the day. I have been catching grasshoppers and thought I'd go catch a fish. How would a big fish taste to you, Berla?"

There wasn't any season on fishing then, nor was a license required. Daddy didn't fish for sport, but for food.

"That would taste good for a change." And then she gasped. While fixing a flag with the yard of red calico and fastening it to a stick, she grabbed the back of a chair and clenched her fists around it. Daddy, busy tying a line to the end of a cane pole, didn't hear the gasp. A hook with a grasshopper fastened to the end of the line was all the equipment needed to catch a big fish. He didn't notice the change in Mama's voice.

"Do you have the horses hooked up? she asked.

"No. I thought I'd just walk up the ditch a way. I'm not going to Flat Creek." Then Daddy picked up a homemade fish bag Mama had made from a flour sack.

"I think you should hook the horses up, Jim—I—"

Daddy looked at her, threw fish bag, line and grasshoppers in the air and ran for the barn so fast Mama didn't have time to change clothes before he had Dan and Bally hitched to Lumber Wagon. Mama called it Lumber Wagon not because of the lumber in it, but because it went lumbering along and never did get them anywhere very fast.

Mama and Mrs. Curtis had decided between them that when Mama took sick she would have Daddy put a red flag

28

up on top of the hill. This would be a signal for Mrs. Curtis to send one of the boys to town on a horse for Dr. Huff, and give her ample time to get a kettle full of boiling water ready, and the sheets changed.

"Hurry!" said Daddy. "I'll lift you up on the bed of hay." He ran for a pillow.

"What about the red flag, dear? It is on the table. I can wait until you climb the hill with it."

"Red flag be hanged," said Daddy. "I'm getting you to the Curtises' then I'll climb the hill and put up the red flag."

Mama grabbed Old Timer off the wall. Time couldn't pass for Mama without Old Timer, then she put a sweater on Margaret. "Here, you take Margaret and I'll make it by myself," she said.

Mama stood the trip very well except for when they had to cross a creek. Daddy was trying to be careful and even Dan and Bally seemed to sense their responsibility. In spite of careful maneuvering, the left front wheel of Lumber Wagon entered the ditch first, then the right front wheel, followed by the left back wheel and then the right back one. This rocked and twisted the wagon in such a manner that Mama felt as if it uncoupled her in several places.

When they arrived there, Mrs. Curtis was in the chicken coop. She heard Daddy say, "Whoa!" She came running out with her apron gathered up in her hands which held a couple dozen eggs.

"Land sakes," she exclaimed. "I didn't see the red flag!" She started running for the house, and in her excitement dropped her apron in order to wave both arms to her son, Lewis, who was just riding off on his horse. "Lewis, Lewis! Oh, my eggs! Lewis, come here quick! Go to town and get Doctor Huff and run your horse every step of the way! Tell him your Ma sent for him and I said Mrs. Chambers is needin' him." She was still screaming as Lewis and his horse rounded the bend out of sight. "Tell him to hurry!

29

Now Jim, get Berla out of that wagon and into the house. I'll change clothes and wash the egg off my shoes." Yelling, toward the house this time, "Ruby, you and Jean get the bed changed in the north bedroom. Get clean sheets out of the bottom drawer! Pearl, get the fire going in the kitchen range, and Hazel, you get several buckets of fresh water from the creek."

The next task was to get the smaller children away from the house. Mr. Curtis instructed Ruby and Hazel to take Arlo and Letha and go stay at the neighbors'. He said he would come for them, but it may be after dark. He looked out in the field and could see Ershel, the eldest son still plowing. The girls rebelled in being rushed out of the house so fast, just when company came. Company was such a treat to anyone living on Flat Creek. Sensing a mystery, they hated to leave more than ever, but no one took time to explain a thing to them.

Lewis was back in an hour with word that Dr. Huff was out on another call, but Lewis had left word with Mrs. Huff to send him right up as soon as he arrived home. Lewis kicked his horse in its flanks and went to the field to help Ershel.

Time dragged for Mama. Daddy and Mrs. Curtis tried to keep a conversation going to help themselves keep calm, but Daddy nearly wore the pattern off the linoleum between Mama's bedroom and the kitchen window, asking how she felt and, at the same time, watching for Doctor Huff.

The boys finished plowing and came in to do the chores. Mr. Curtis jumped on the saddle horse and rode to the neighbors' to explain the situation and see if the two smaller children could stay all night.

About nine o'clock, Dr. Huff arrived. Daddy had been listening and watching through the dusk to be ready to greet him. The doctor jumped from the buggy, threw Daddy the lines, grabbed his little black bag, which was on the seat beside him, and ran to the house with it.

"She's doing just fine, James," he said as he came from Mama's bedroom. "I'm not going to be needed here for several hours and I have another woman needing me, so I'll go back to town and return here early in the morning."

Feeling a sudden burst of resentfulness, Daddy said, "You can't leave my wife, Doc. She has been sick for—" Pulling his watch from his bib overalls, "nine or ten hours now. She's nearly worn out."

"I know James, but it is always harder on the fathers than the mothers. I must serve all humanity to the best of my ability! I'll be back."

Doctor Huff was a large man who carried himself straight. He wore a small, neatly trimmed mustache to cover a scar on his upper lip. His English was that of a well-educated man, and even though he was a country doctor, he never let down in character even for a minute. Everyone respected him and his education.

Doctor Huff made three trips to that ranch to see Mama. He had brought two babies into the world in the meantime. The third time he left, which was three days after Mama had first arrived at the Curtis ranch, he promised to be back in about five hours. That was daylight on Saturday morning.

At 9:30 a.m., Mama called Mrs. Curtis and said, "Can you see Dr. Huff coming? I need him quick."

Daddy was sitting at her bedside holding her hand. He ran to the window, but seeing nothing of the Doctor, ran outside. Mr. Curtis followed.

Wondering what to do next, Daddy stood with his hand on his forehead, shading his eyes and looking as far in the distance as he could.

Mr. Curtis put his hand on Daddy's shoulder and assured him, "Don't worry, Jim! My wife has had nine children and will know what to do for your wife."

The men turned and walked back into the house and

found Mrs. Curtis had fainted and fallen on the floor.

In a pleading voice, Mama said, "Jim, do something! I can wait no longer."

Daddy did do something. He stood in the middle of the floor and wrung his hands.

Mr. Curtis, a big strong, sturdy man, with a husky body, always spoke in a slow, low, whispering, voice and nothing ever excited him too much. Asking permission from Daddy, he said while rubbing his hands together, "Jim, if you don't mind, I'll scrub up a bit and pretend I'm the doctor. I think I can do it."

Daddy gave his permission readily, then ran for a cup of cold water to revive Mrs. Curtis.

Dr. Huff arrived back at the ranch at 10:10, just ten minutes too late. All was quiet. both men had stepped outside to greet him, but did not break the news. Mrs. Curtis was standing beside Mama's bed when the doctor burst into the room. He rushed to Mama, threw back the covers, gasped, looked at Mrs. Curtis' pale face, sucked in another deep breath and—looked at ME. He kneeled beside Mama's bed, spit on the end of his pointer finger and parted my long black hair from my eyes.

A job well done, Mrs. Curtis, and a fine baby girl for you Mrs. Chambers, Doctor Huff said, at the same time apologizing as to why he had been detained. "Let's weigh her," he said, as he lifted my red, squirmy body to the scales. "A fine big baby indeed. She weighs exactly ten pounds."

Taking me from him, Mrs. Curtis wrapped me in the soft, pink blanket from the mail-order catalog.

While Mama, Margaret and I spent the next fifteen days at the Curtis home, we were well-entertained. They had a phonograph—the kind that had to be hand wound when it ran down. They had one record in the house. It had been played so many times the grooves were well worn. From Mama's room she got the full benefit from both sides of the record. One side played "The Bear Went Over The Mountain." The other side was all about "Uncle Josh Churning Butter." When he took the lid off the churn to see if he had butter, he dropped his tobacco in the churn. He didn't care about the butter, but it was all the tobacco he had. Mama wished many times she could get out of bed and go to town to buy Uncle Josh a plug of tobacco, if it would shut him up. She also wished that bear would get lost over the mountain so far they couldn't find the mountain he was lost on.

When we all arrived home, we had lots of visitors the first week. Grandma McInelly came with a new apron for Mama and a new bonnet for me. Mrs. Goe said she just had to come see Mama's new baby and to show off her own baby girl. She brought a cake. She and Mama had lots of fun talking names that afternoon, and comparing babies and she said she and her husband liked the name of Alice Louise. My name had been chosen a long time ago, but somehow, James Jr. didn't seem to fit me now. My name caused more discussion and disagreements than Daddy and Mama had ever had before in their married life.

One day, Daddy came in from the field all out of breath. "Babs, I have thought of the name I want our baby girl called."

Raising her eyebrow and cocking her head to one side, Mama said, "Oh! What is it this time?"

"Elzada," said Daddy. "I used to have a girlfriend by—"

Mama stopped him right there. "Girl friend or no girl friend, I'll never give my pretty baby girl an ugly name like that."

"Let's see you come up with a better one," Daddy said.

"All right!" Mama shouted. "Calperna."

Daddy fell down on the floor and rolled with laughter.

"Oh, get up Jim. You look like old Bally when he gets his harness off," Mama said in a disgusted voice.

Since being such a big baby to begin with, Mama thought I was going to be half grown before given a name. The day came for my christening. Mama wanted me called Myra and Daddy was holding out for Rhea. They decided to flip a coin. Heads, I would be Rhea, tails, I would be Myra. Daddy flipped a quarter. It rolled under the wash stand. Mama pulled it out. It came up heads. She sat there and tears fell from her eyes, but she dressed me in my pretty, long, white christening dress she had made for the special occasion, put me in a white shawl, Margaret in a pink dress, and announced to Daddy, "We are ready to leave for the church."

Dr. Charles W. Huff

On the way there, Daddy whistled a merry little tune. Mama kept glancing over to him out of the corner of her eye. "He seems to be happy about this, but even though I'm not happy, I'll go along with it."

Almost reading her thoughts, he reached over and patted her hand. "Honey, in your mind, something still seems to be pending. Let's compromise! Let's name her after your twin sister and put the two names of Myra and Rhea together with it.

"What kind of a name would Bertha Myra Rhea be?" she asked.

Daddy laughed and said, "I mean make one word out of Myra and Rhea."

Mama smiled and patted Daddy's hand and peeked down in the blankets at me and asked. "How would you like that, my dear?" I must have grinned or something, because I was christened Bertha Myrea.

Chapter V
THE HOLE IN THE MOUNTAIN

Much to the surprise of many people of the Jackson Hole territory and more so to Mrs. Robert (Grace) Miller, it was announced by a phone call to Mrs. Miller one morning that in a caucus meeting the night before she had been nominated to run on the city board as Mayor.

At first, Mrs. Miller thought someone was playing a joke on her and never was sure it wasn't started as a joke. Of course, she laughed and said, "Oh, no. I'm not going to let anyone make a fool out of me like that."

The voice on the other end of the line assured her he was in earnest and said they discussed, in the meeting, "Why not put women in and see if we can get a few things done."

Mrs. Miller gasped and pulled a chair over and sat down. "I'll talk it over with Rob. —No, he would only think I'm joking. I'll talk it over with—no, maybe I'll just think it over for awhile."

"I'll call you back in an hour," the voice said.

In a few weeks, Mrs. Grace Miller was elected Mayor of Jackson. Her councilwomen were Mrs. Mae Deloney, Mrs. Rose Crabtree, and Mrs. Faustina Haight and Mrs. Genevieve Van Vleck. Mrs. Martha Winger was elected clerk; Mrs. Viola Lunbeck Treasurer, and Pearl Williams, Marshall.

These women never failed to have a monthly council meeting. During the three years they were in office, the city park was beautified, the streets improved and a title was secured for the city cemetery. The cemetery was surveyed and platted and a road built to it.

Not only did they get full support from their husbands, but also the general public. It gave Jackson, Wyoming the distinguished honor of being the first town in the United States to be governed by women. They were happy, cheerful, and served the city well.

By this time, many more people had taken up "Squatter's Rights." We had neighbors all around us. Even though they varied in ancestry, they blended as well as the colors of the rainbow.

One of the oddities about each newcomer was that he felt he had made a personal, virtuous, discovery, and set about improving what he felt to be the most scenic portion of Flat Creek.

We watched people arrive and adapt themselves to an ambitious way of life, clearing virgin soil, planting roots as if they planned on spending all the rest of their days on Flat Creek, in the Jackson Hole Country, making new acquaintances and helping their neighbors. No one could deny that each man was doing a man-sized job, wasting no time in preparing his ground for future development, which later would be a historic landmark in Old West history. Even though they found it easy to detect faults about the new country, at the same time, they found ways and means to abstract the difficulties and speak convincingly that they knew this land would prosper.

Olivette Webb, a beautiful young school teacher had come in from Idaho to visit her aunts, Maggy McBride and Josephine Saunders. This delighted many Flat Creek folks as there were two eligible young bachelors seeking a wife. George Goe was the lucky young man who coaxed her to stay in the country to become his bride. She decided to stay to teach the Cheney school that winter while making up her mind. In the spring, she married George and moved with him to the ranch on Flat Creek, formerly owned by Mr. Lanigan.

Truly an excited young bride, she moved into the two room cabin which offered her a real challenge. She vigorously tore the old newspaper from the walls, repapered with new paper, made dainty curtains for the windows, scrubbed the bare floor to a shine, blackened the cook stove with polish, and before long her home was a gay little cottage. "Nothing in the world could be more thrilling," Olivette said, as she put the finishing touches to her little abode.

Soon, George added two more rooms from logs he got from the nearby hills. Olivette made rag carpets for these old rooms, but what could she do for the new? The answer was obvious. She remembered seeing some old factory material on a cabin her husband lived in before they were married and now wasn't being used. She went to the cabin, removed the factory, washed and dyed it brown and wove it into a carpet. When it showed signs of wearing, she stretched and tacked it down, painted it with several coats of brown paint, then she called it her linoleum rug.

In this humble abode, four of her children were born. The eldest child, a boy, died when three days old. Thornley, Meredith, and Ninabeth grew up with the rest of the Flat Creek children and called this land "Blessed."

To the northwest of us lived an old bachelor. He never attended any of the Flat Creek reunions, nor was he ever seen in any other public gathering. No one knew his age, including himself. He had been a stow-away on a ship from Austria when a very young lad. How he ever got to Flat Creek to settle no one ever knew. And when he wanted to leave his ranch, he either did so on a fat, sorrel, work horse or on a pair of homemade skis he had hewn from two tree trunks. He fashioned harnesses for his skis from scraps of leather. He came to visit us about two or three times a year, but did visit the Petersens a few more times than that since he lived close to them. The rest of the Flat Creek folks hardly knew he existed. He was very short in stature, had a lean, wiry, frame and was very lively for an old man. This much people did know about his age; he was the oldest man on Flat Creek. His gray hair hung long, down into his shirt collar. He wore octagon shaped glasses, the same pair all his life, and when they became so dirty he could no longer see through them, he wiped them with his bare hands, causing a smudge across both lenses. He carried a wooden leg, and with the aid of a cane walked with a decided limp, shifting his body way low on the right side and high on the left.

One day, Daddy and Mr. Petersen learned that he had a prize rooster. You could talk Mr. Ritter out of almost anything he owned, except for his horse, his homemade skis, his cane, and that prize rooster. But of the four, he was most vainglorious of the rooster.

Daddy and Mr. Petersen would get together and ride over to Mr. Ritter's place just to tease him about the rooster. They tried trading him tools, lumber, grain, and even their wives for the bird, but he wouldn't talk. If he didn't want to listen he had a way of letting one know he couldn't understand the language.

He never did get his citizenship papers, but no one needed to be a citizen, so long as he lived on Flat Creek. Just call anyone living there a settler, or an old timer, he became everyone's friend, and all the neighbors welcomed him.

One day, Mr. Ritter made it known that his real name was George Geislaritter. He seemed to sense the fact that no American could ever be able to twist his tongue in a manner to pronounce the whole name correctly, so he dropped the first few syllables.

Daddy stood in the doorway one morning and saw Mr. Ritter jogging forward and backward on his horse with his wooden leg dangling out of the stirrup. The horse was traveling at a slow, deliberate, forceful, speed. He stepped out in the yard to greet him and saw Mr. Ritter crying. Daddy tried to get him to tell his troubles. This queer little man was hard to understand at his best; worse when feeling so badly. Daddy thought perhaps one of his relatives had passed away. Finally he stopped his stammering, climbed off his horse, tied him to a post, then said, "Mr. Chambers, my old prize rooster died yesterday."

Daddy started to sympathize with him. "That's too bad! What caused his death?"

"I don't know," he said. "Just got sick and died. It's nice of you to say kind words sir," then wiping his sleeve across his nose and managing a smile, "But the joke was on the rooster, 'cause I eat him anyway."

Around the point of the hill and to the southeast of us, in the heart of the hills, lived an old maid neighbor who was about thirty when she came to Flat Creek. It didn't seem to be very clear in anyone's mind just where she came from, nor exactly when she started "Squatter's Rights." Very few people ever entered her homestead. She had a gun and whenever anyone came close to her property she started shooting. Finally people learned that she had settled back in the hills where she did for bootleg purposes. She had a homemade still and made "moonshine." Her home was well-camouflaged by brush and trees and few people knew it was there. She would go to town on a horse, let a few men whom she knew in on her secret, and then explain to them that only steady customers would be allowed to enter her premises. She could tell her customers from intruders or law enforcers. She lived between our place and the Curtis ranch, but with no road between us.

We had a place on our ranch we called "The Draw." It was a passageway between two mountains, through which we took our cows to and from pasture each summer day. Had Mama and Daddy not put the fear of all fears into their children about guns, we may have gone back through the draw at some time or other far enough to have seen her and her house, but so long as she lived there, I only saw her from a distance while riding her horse to town or back.

A great lover of cats, she owned them by the hundreds. For food for them she killed an elk. When they had eaten it, she would kill another one.

A couple of men rode up to her place one day to buy

some "moonshine" and found her in bed very ill. She called to them. "Come in," in a voice so weak she could hardly speak. They asked her if they should have Dr. Huff come see her, but she insisted she would get better in a few days. She had some of her own "shine" on a stand beside her bed, this being all the medicine or nourishment she had taken for days. She left her door open so her cats could come and go as they pleased. There were so many cats in her house, on her bed, in the cupboards and all over the place that the men became worried. When they arrived back in town, they contacted Dr. Huff and he said, "Why, she will get so weak lying there alone, and the cats may get so hungry that they may devour her." Dr. Huff promised the men he would go up for her and take her to the hospital. He did, and she never returned to her home and her cats.

Almost directly west of us, past the swamps, lived Mr. and Mrs. Joe Infinger, and their two sons, John and Joe Jr. Young Joe was sickly most of his life and died when a very young boy. Mr. Infinger passed away shortly afterwards.

John, a healthy young man, trapped mink and martin alive, raised them to maturity and sold them for furs. These little animals gave the Infinger ranch a capricious personality.

We enjoyed visiting Mrs. Infinger while Daddy and John seined whitefish. The tantalizing part was the waiting for days for the fish to come forth from John's smokehouse, cured and smoked to a golden brown. Mr. and Mrs. Infinger came from The Old Country, and she had many interesting stories to tell us. John always showed patience with us children and let us help feed his queer little animals. The Infingers were some of our finest neighbors, always having machinery, tools and good ideas to lend.

When John started courting the girls, Mrs. Infinger went along, taking her usual place in the front seat beside "Yonny," as she always called him.

41

"No sassy young t'ing is going to take my place," she once told Mama. The girl had to take the back seat.

Long after everyone else on Flat Creek had his property all improved, an impecunious family came in and settled to the northeast of us. That land was full of alkali and nothing could grow on it. Mr. Pearl Summers and his wife settled there first, built a home, and stayed until they had one boy, Percy, then left, since they could see no future for them there.

This family who came later was named Hutters. They had no home before coming to Flat Creek, but had been on the move for three years, killing wild game for food and lodging in any building available along the way.

They stopped at our house one hot summer day inquiring for work. Daddy told them about the empty house beyond us. It didn't take them long to move in for they only had one team of horses, one wagon, a gun, a bundle of bedding, a few kettles, an old trunk, a worn out tent, three children, an irresponsible father, and a sick mother. The daughter, Bessie, a beautiful girl, twelve years old and very intelligent, tried ever so hard to make friends with everyone. Her brother, older than she, a tall, gawky, long-legged boy of sixteen, had only gone through the fourth grade. He loved to paint with oils and spent many hours so doing. The little boy, eight years of age, was very witty, and could wiggle his ears. All the family looked emaciated. They existed on field rabbits, tree squirrels, and ravens. Since we had a garden, the two boys nearly lived at our house. They would come to see us early in the morning and stay until dark. They offered to weed the garden for a few vegetables. Maurice, the older one, would say at mealtime, "Come on Bobart, pull your chair right up here by mine. I'll move over and let you in."

Mama loved these children and tried to make them feel welcome, even though she felt that Maurice was a little voracious, but would often laugh about them after they had gone. "People like they are to be more pitied than censured," she would say.

The Hutters children attended Flat Creek school one winter. All three of them rode one of the skinny, poor, and windbroken work horses, About ten minutes after the bell had rung each morning, we could see them bouncing on the horse; Maurice flogging it, first on one side then the other, with a rope. The horse could be heard breathing as far as it could be seen. Every day, Bessie tried to trade one of her crow sandwiches for one of ours made with jam, chicken, or elk.

The Hutters only stayed one summer and one winter. Mr. Hutters got lazier, and Mrs. Hutters got sicker, so they moved on.

Another man moved into the place after the Hutters moved out. He brought with him a cow, a horse and a few chickens. A few days after he moved there, Daddy came in with a bucket of milk and said to Mama. "Berla, strain this milk then let's take the children and go for a little walk and get acquainted with our new neighbor."

Shadows lengthening and the sinking of the sun behind the Tetons cast a red glow on the east mountains.

"That's what I love about this Flat Creek territory," Mama said. "Its indescribable beauty is forever changing. look at Sheep Mountain. I don't think I have ever seen it more beautiful." She pointed out to us, as we walked toward it, the outline of Sheep Mountain which looked like an old Indian Chief lying on his back with his nose in the air and his feather head dress resting on a pillow.

"How long did it take God to make the old Indian?" I asked.

"Eons of time," replied Mama.

As we approached our neighbor's place, we saw him coming out of the barn with part of a pail of milk in one hand

and two funny looking things in the other. He didn't see us at first, and went right on cursing. Daddy stepped in front of all of us, gave us a shove with his hand, as if to protect us from some wild creature. Daddy introduced himself, Mama, and us children and then asked his name.

"Just call me Jess," he said. He was wearing an old pair of faded bib overalls, a gray turtleneck sweater, high work shoes and a red face. He started stammering and apologizing for the language he had been using in the barn. He told the funniest and yet the most sympathetic story I had ever heard.

"It isn't often I cuss so, but I am overwrought. I started milking this here cow, and she had a sore teat and wouldn't stand still. I tried to calm her, but no how could I do it. She wouldn't stand for nothin.' She switched her old tail across my face, kicked the stool out from under me, then kicked the bucket of milk over. By that time, I was so furious I saw stars. Then she slapped me across the kisser again with her tail. I had enough so I looked for a club and decided to beat her to death. I couldn't find a stick of any kind, but up above me on a pole sat the old rooster. I grabbed him by his two hind legs and I let that cow have it. I beat her so hard with that rooster she was mooin' and beggin' me to take pity on her. That poor bird wondered what in this world he was doin' that made me take my spite out on him like that. This is all there was left of the chicken when I got through beatin' that cow." He showed us the two legs he still held in his shaking hand.

He tossed the stubs into the air, and they lit on top of the barn. He put his pail on a stump then ran his hand through his mop of ash-blonde hair and said, "Mighty glad to meet chu. I buried my wife two weeks ago. She was all I had. I hain't got no children nor no other livin' relatives. I wanted to run away from my troubles, so I headed out here."

No one really seemed to own the land, nor did anyone

care who moved into the place, nor moved out.

We didn't stay long, and as we left, Mama invited him down for supper some evening. She knew what lonely hours one could spend on Flat Creek alone.

When we reached home, twilight was falling and only a silver outline could be seen above the Tetons.

Arriving a little later than some of the Flat Creek folks, a man and his beautiful bride settled northeast, beyond most of the settlers. Walter and Bertha Scott built a tiny log house, the necessary few outbuildings, and struggled with the rest to make the sagebrush flat flourish. They toiled and planned for more prosperous days, but thought, "Even with more money, we could never be happier."

On the day they arrived, they stopped their horses and buggy, chatting with several farmers, asking which direction would be the best to go. They kept traveling until they came to the mouth of Dry Hollow. They could see this had to be the end of their journey as the territory narrowed down into a deep canyon, and it was as far as they could go on wheels.

"Whoa!" commanded Walter. Then, looking around him for a perplexing moment, "See right over there honey! If the best man on earth would erect a house on that little knoll, do you think you could be happy with him in it, and have a desire to call it home?"

A big white cloud hovered overhead, causing a cool-looking shadow to descend upon the knoll.

"Darlin', I could live anywhere on this earth and be happy with you. This looks to me like the most completely satisfyin' place on the whole wide continent, so start buildin' while the sun shines in the valley and the shadow's on the knoll."

Here the sagebrush had faded out, to be replaced with angel-white sego lilies, and other wild flowers in season.

While they lived in their humble home, two lovely

children came to bless it. The daughter they named Winonia, and the son Lawrence.

During one wintery night, a heavy feeling came over Walter and he started coughing. By morning, he could hardly speak. His pretty wife tenderly nursed him, but he became weaker. He managed to hook his horses to the sleigh several days later, and he drove to town to see Dr. Huff.

"Influenza!" the doctor said, as he looked down Walter's throat and listened to his chest. "Now, take this prescription over to the druggist. I'm sorry I don't have room for you here in the hospital, but all ten beds are full. This influenza has turned into an epidemic. Whatever you do, don't go home! You will give this germ to your wife and when she gets it, she will lose her baby and you may even lose her. Expectant mothers cannot endure this." Then putting his hand on Walter's arm, helped him to his feet. "Good luck Mr. Scott and take all the pills I prescribe.

Poor Walter! Where else did he have to go but home? Bertha, so patient and kind, did all she could for him. Both children took ill and she watched over and nursed them the same as she did her husband.

After several days, she had them all back to health, but by then the germ had hit her. She started to cough and this caused a hemorrhage. A tiny, premature baby boy was stillborn. The neighbors around either had the flu or were too frightened to offer any assistance. For a few days, Mrs. Scott laid so weak she couldn't move.

"Does the noise of the children bother you dear?" her husband asked as he tried to lift her head to give her a cool drink. Fever seemed to be burning every inch of her body.

She could barely whisper, "No, let them play, they do not realize the situation."

She suffered no pain, just kept getting weaker and succumbed on the twenty-eighth day of December.

Her home had been in Utah where her parents lived. Walter decided to take the body there for burial. He left the two children with George and Olivette Goe for three weeks. He took the body in a sleigh over the Teton Pass and on to St. Anthony, Idaho to the nearest undertaker, then shipped it to Utah for burial. The funeral was held in the yard of her parents' home and no one came near the casket for fear of the influenza germ.

Upon arriving back home, Walter took his two children with him and returned to an empty house. He went to the woodshed for fire material and there found the unforgotten body of the infant son, frozen stiff. With tearstained cheeks, he took his shovel and pick, dug a shallow grave in the frozen earth and laid the babe to rest.

Away up and beyond all other settlers places, even above the Scotts', Flat Creek headed from a glacier which trickled from the mountains and formed a lake. From that outlet flowed Flat Creek. At this spot was some land owned by a very wealthy Countess. She settled there all alone, except for a saddle horse. She loved the exotic beauty of the rugged gorges and lush, green, padded meadows where she watched deer grazing or drinking at a stream. "This is Paradise," she thought. She had had a beautiful court built, surrounded by log buildings. From the lodge where she lived, she could look out over the lake, and see the water dotted with waterfowls. She could travel the many trails into the woods, made by deer, elk, and other animals as they came down to the lake to drink, and was not afraid of the vastness of the great out-of-doors. She loved every wonder-work of nature.

The Countess enjoyed swimming in the lake, or rowing upon it in a canoe. Indeed she seemed happy until the fall winds started to blow down from the canyon. She walked out one day to the edge of the lake and listened. The wind sounded to her like the urgent whisper of wire brushes beating on a slightly loosened, soft-headed drum. She watched the sands on the lake shore erase the tidal wave marks and knew for a surety winter was coming in spite of the serenity she had known that summer.

That night was a long one for her, and before morning, the winds had drummed up a big roar. The next few days she spent boarding up doors and windows, padlocking all the out buildings, putting away everything she could in preparation for winter at "The Hole In The Mountain." In less than a week, the snows came.

"I'm not afraid," she bolstered herself. "I have plenty of wood, fuel, and bedding. I shall want for nothing. This solitude is exactly what I need. I'm tired of being a celebrity."

What the Countess didn't know was that winter on Flat Creek lasted seven months, and at The Hole In The Mountain, it lasted nine. She hadn't thought what might happen should she take sick.

Carefully, she kept a diary for the first month, telling about the deer and elk dutifully leading their spring-born calves to the lake for water. Filling the first few pages with detailed happenings, her diary entries grew briefer, and finally like the sunsets of last summer, quietly died away.

By December, she couldn't see out any window in her mansion. She melted snow for water for herself and the horse, and kept a scoop shovel inside her door so she could dig her way out of her snow-bound house to the barn to feed her horse.

When spring finally came, she was thin and wan from worry, but brave enough, when ice had broken up into chunks on the lake, to stand on the still snowy bank and utter, "The sky is brilliantly blue; this air is incredibly exhilarating, and I'm glad I stayed here and wintered the worse."

Going back into her house, she took the calendar from

a nail on the kitchen wall, carefully tore off the pages from September through May, shuffled them through her fingers and saw where she had marked off each day before going to bed. Remembering how she had counted days both backward and forward, wondering when she had reached the middle, folded the pages together then said, "This is my evidence. I shall keep this as a lasting souvenir."

The summer days were welcomed, but even they grew monotonous and long before another fall when winds drummed up blasts of snow flurries. The Countess decided she needed a caretaker to leave at her place the year around, but being unable to find a man, she boarded her buildings again, including the lodge, and left "The Hole In The Mountain."

The next spring when she returned she brought with her a jolly, lanky, young man, as rigid and sound as a stake of iron. He was never known to be without a broad smile—not just a grin, but an honest-to-goodness healthy smile, which made his mouth look as if it had been seamed that way. His name was Cal Carrington. He became the Countess' hired man, her horseman, her fixer-upper, and tearer-downer. He added beauty to her place by building bird houses, tacking them on tall poles, the corners of buildings, and gate posts. He proved to be such good help and companion to the Countess, she took Cal with her when she left each fall.

One day, while in town, someone told her about a bachelor she could probably hire to stay at her place during the winters.

Forney Cole was tongue-tied and bashful, but not the kind who would ever get lonely. He weighed about one hundred and eighty five pounds, had a swarthy skin, and long, bushy hair stuck out at his throat from under his shirt collar.

The Countess had bought a year's supply of groceries for him and paid him a wage.

49

Forney worked hard to try to find enough to do to keep his hands and mind occupied. He scraped the side of the mountain away, leveling dirt and planting flowers and shrubs he knew could flourish in that difficult climate. He cultured the wild flowers already growing there—violets, bluebells, grandpa whiskers, and trilliums. Aside from all this, it was a fine excuse to meander in the great outdoors he loved so well. Often in the early spring, while raking and working among the dead leaves, he gathered timber mushrooms, sauted them in butter and relished their delicate flavor.

He decided one day to go out into the woods close by and chop down some Aspen trees, peel them, and make a fence to go around the yard. He worked early and late for several days and nearly had the job completed when he heard a growl and there right before him stood a big, brown bear, with thick hair standing up on his back, and the tip of his hair glistening in the sun like silver swords. This bear was angry and Forney didn't have time to try to figure out why. Reaching for his ax he found it closer to the bear than to him. Forney had heard the tale that if one would fall down and pretend dead when being attacked by a bear, it would go away and leave him alone. He tried this. He fell down as close to a big dead log as he could. Bruin pawed his way over to him, growling with every step. Forney's heart was beating so loud that that bear couldn't help but know there was life in that body. He reached out and tried to pry Forney away from the log. Forney decided it would be better to roll away than to be pawed away, so he turned over very willingly. Bruin slapped his face to awaken him. The blood spurted from the claw marks and the flesh of his face hung in strips. He came to life, grabbed an Aspen branch and proceeded to show that bear who was boss of that territory.

Growling furiously with every swap, the bear was winning for a long time. He tore the clothes from Forney's body, clawed deep into the flesh on his shoulders, but just when Bruin made what both he and Forney thought would be the last plunge, Forney stuck the vital blow across the head with the club. The bear laid there with his eyes still wide open, puffing and panting with every breath.

Forney stood staggering, mighty weak, but he finished the fight with just that club and his bare, bleeding hands.

He dragged his weary torn body to the house, bathed his wounds with hot water, and several days passed before he felt strong enough to get off his bed to saddle his horse and go see the doctor. He knew he had to see Dr. Huff or die from blood poisoning. He managed to saddle his horse, but to get upon him looked like an impossible task. His legs were so sore they couldn't lift him into the saddle. He led his horse to a bank of dirt, climbed upon it, and reached his saddle stirrup from there.

Feeling mighty sick, he didn't stop along the way to tell a neighbor, but kept going until he reached Dr. Huff's place. Forney carried those scars to his grave. He had plenty of witness from them, a blood-stained club, and a dead bear, to show that he had been numbered among the fortunate.

As soon as Forney was able he went back to "The Hole In The Mountain," determined that neither bear nor beast would ever get the best of him again. He lived there and tended the place for the Countess for many years. He went to town about three or four times a year, on his fat horse, and told many weird tales about how the mountains rolled, the awesome winds howled and warned him of danger, and how he heard strange cries from animals which he couldn't recognize.

In his excitement, his tongue refused to cooperate with him mind, but the people in town could tell from the expression on his face, the disturbance in his eyes, and the quivering of his body that he was completely overwrought. Some kind-hearted soul would always invite him to come

51

stay at his home a day or so until he could be talked out of this morbid condition. After about three days in town, he became calm enough to talk a bit. Each time he told the same horrifying tale. In his tongue-tied manner, he told how these noises thundered through the mountains, the animals shrieked and screamed, and his bed walked all over the room.

Above all, he wanted people to believe in him, and he took pride in being trusted—but after a few days visiting in town he began to believe what people were saying about him losing his mind was true. He decided to show people he could go up there and this time he would stick it out.

One day, Forney came out of the mountains on his horse with his bedroll and clothing. He avowed he would never go back. He hired the postmaster to write a letter to the Countess as he could neither read nor write. He told her he was a sick man, that his mind was failing him. He told her he had locked every door of every building with a padlock and would gladly turn the keys over to anyone.

About a month later, the Countess hired a man by the name of Bob Stanton to be the caretaker. Stanton was also a bachelor. The Countess couldn't find a married couple to go there as no woman alive could take that loneliness, tension and solitude.

Stanton was very hard of hearing, a steady, easy going soul with a strong physique, and constitution, and not possessed with autophobia. His hair was as white as January frost, and he believed that if Sampson, in the Bible, got strength from letting his hair grow, so could he. His hair reached his shoulders.

Taking his white mare, a roll of bedding and a few clothes, he departed for "The Hole In The Mountain," whistling as he wavered in his saddle.

Late in October then, no one saw him until the spring thaws were over. People began to wonder about Stanton, but knew it was almost a physical impossibility to get to him. In the spring of the year, floods rolled forth from the mountains, streams of water ran down the gullies, and Flat Creek raised to its brinks.

One day, late in April, Stanton passed through the Flat Creek Territory, swinging, swaying and singing in the saddle, on his way to town. Each neighbor along the way stopped him to ask if he had heard any "funny, rumbling noises" during the winter months there. As he was so hard of hearing, their messages and questions had to be written. Stanton carried a notebook and pencil for such purposes. He laughed each time, shook his head and said, "Nay, I nerry heerd a thing, but once in a while I did feel my bed walkin' across the floor."

He got some provisions at the little brick store, charged them to the Countess, put his horse in the livery stable, and got a room at the hotel in order to get an early start back the next morning.

About two months later, midday in June, here came Stanton and the white mare, a fog of dirt flying behind them. The mare was all out of breath, and so was Stanton. Daddy was working close to the road, picking rocks off his land, and motioned for Stanton to stop.

Stanton waved his arms and shouted, "There's ghosts in them hills and they're after me." Daddy tried to shout to him to ask him what he saw or heard to frighten him. Stanton finally said, "I didn't hear a thing, but I saw and felt a plenty."

The Countess got another letter. This time, she tried for three months and finally hired Mr. Ritter, the old Austrian bachelor, with the octagon shaped glasses.

Mr. Ritter took his fat horse, a roll of bedding and a few clothes and departed for the Countess' "Hole In The Mountain."

In one little section of Flat Creek stood the little school

house. It consisted of one room with a partition made of white sheets in one corner. Behind that partition, Mrs. Saunders lived five days out of the week, then went to town to her home on weekends. In those tiny quarters, she had a bed, a small table, one chair and an orange crate to hold her dishes. All eight grades were taught in one room, but not only did the teacher teach us, she also acted as janitor, nurse maid, and counselor. Sometimes, she taught as many as fourteen students. One year, she only had five. Four of them were we Chambers children and the other was Martha Petersen.

One day soon after school had started in September, Mr. Ritter rode up on his horse to the porch, tied the horse to the post and asked Mrs. Saunders if he could come in. This was recess time and all we children were playing down in the dell, under the hill, where we rolled down in a barrel or on a homemade cart.

Of course, Mrs. Saunders invited Mr. Ritter to come in. He raved on like a mad man in his foreign tongue and Mrs. Saunders couldn't' tell a word he was saying. She became so frightened she rang the bell five minutes early so we would come in and be with her. We were unaware of a visitor, until we saw the horse, so he was greeted with the usual eruption, characteristic of children. At first we were captivated by a visitor, but settled in our seats for further instructions from our teacher.

About the time we all were quiet and studying, Mr. Ritter started shouting again. "My furniture she walked all over the room." As he got down on the floor and rolled, putting on a demonstration in the aisles, between the desks, we laughed until some of us almost became hysterical. We were obviously amused by his actions while trying to keep his wooden leg in the right place at the right time. Mrs. Saunders stood perplexed, near the open door and finally got him on his feet then began encouraging him to ride over to Mr. Petersen's to tell the story to him.

The rumor spread around that Mr. Ritter had lost his mind.

He returned to the Countess', but almost regularly once a week he visited the Petersens with more weird tales.

Some of the men around Flat Creek rode up there one day with Mr. Ritter to see if they could detect why these men each lost his mind. They came to the conclusion that the loneliness about the place would make anyone of them placed there for one month alone, go crazy.

The men of Flat Creek wrote a letter to the Countess, Daddy acting as scribe, and explained to her that she should do one of two things, either dispose of her property or build a big road back there which wagons could travel, then build more homes and hire more people. Maybe she could get two couples to live there then.

Mr. Ritter became old and ill so fast that Dr. Huff made arrangements for him to be taken to a rest home for old people, where he soon passed away. He was the last caretaker ever to live at the Countess' "Hole In The Mountain."

The next February the people of Flat Creek and people for miles around learned what had made three men nearly lose their minds.

It happened during the night when the thermometers went to forty below zero. A thundering, roaring, whooing, sound rolled out of the mountains from the direction of the Countess'.

"It sounded and felt as if all Hell had torn loose," one of our neighbors said later.

The earth rocked, rolled, heaved and twisted. Every bed, in every man's house on Flat Creek rolled across the floor and back again. The animals, both tame and wild cried and shrieked. The chickens flew around until the floor of the coops were covered with feathers. This was an earthquake like no one living on Flat Creek had ever witnessed before.

The neighbors knew now that these three men had been experiencing tremors previous to this big one.

Several days later, Daddy and Mr. Goe went to the top of Sheep Mountain. Scaling a mountain as large as this one, on webs, was no easy task, but they reached the summit about noon. They could still hear roars and rumbles which sounded as if the noises were rolling forth from a deep cave. As they webbed over the top of the mountain they discovered a place which had cracked wide open, leaving a crevasse twelve feet wide and many feet deep. They knew then the torture the three lonely men had gone through for many years alone while staying at "The Hole In The Mountain."

Flat Creek School House

Chapter VI

TO THE TOP OF THE TETONS

"Why don't you cook up something different today," Daddy asked Mama one Sunday morning. "Put a little fancy touch to it, and I'll ride over to the Petersens and ask them to come to dinner."

"Now, Sir Hon," Mama replied, "I would love to have company come, but the only way I can make elk meat taste different is to sprinkle it with a little garlic salt."

"Well, do your best and I'll be back shortly."

We children could hardly wait. Charlie, Frankie and Martha would be coming, too. Leonard had long since been gone from home.

"Get in the bottom of the trunk, girls, and get the linen tablecloth—the one we use for Thangsgiving," Mama said, "and Margaret, here, you take this package of soda, put a little in a dish and make some paste of it and water, and try to polish the silverware a bit. It's awfully old and tarnished, but it's the best we have."

"I have never eaten such good meat in all my life!" exclaimed Mrs. Petersen at the dinner table. "What do you call this, Berla?"

Laughingly Mama said, "I call it Shanty roast, for lack of a better name."

"And your biscuits taste even better than the sourdough biscuits Billy Owen stirred up and cooked in a frying pan the time we climbed to the top of the Grand Teton," Mr. Petersen said. Then, taking his napkin, he wiped his mouth and chuckled.

"I always wanted to hear that story, Frank," said Daddy, "and I'm sure the Mrs. and the kids will enjoy it too. Let's take our chairs and go in the other room and listen to this story."

"Go on in and get seated while I clear the table and put

the dishes to soak," Mama chimed in.

"It isn't every man who has a particular yen to climb the heights," said Mr. Petersen as he sat down, "but somehow Billy Owen stirred this desire in Jack Shives and me. At first, when we began talking about climbing the Grand, it grew from an idea to a desire; then for a whole week just before making our departure for the ascent, I awoke every morning with the unshakable conviction I really wanted to reach the top of that mountain more than anything else in the world. We then convinced Mr. Cooper.

"We were young troupers, healthy, sturdy, and robust, and with our determination we prevailed against the many people who tried to discourage us.

"We knew the journey would be a hazardous one, and that to return home safely was questionable.

"It took us about three months to prepare our pack, which consisted of special climbing tools, shoes, ropes, food, canvas, utensils and bedding.

"In the days to follow, we took every precaution possible. The first day we walked slowly and steadily up the long slope. We stopped to eat by a glacier stream just below the timberline. After eating lunch we followed the stream a short distance, then turned to our right and proceeded up Garnet Canyon. We walked along the top of the moraine made by the glacier centuries ago. Here we could look down into the deep crevasses, and as we stopped now and then to catch our breath we heard echoes and muffled roars from the canyon walls.

"Sheltered by a large rock we spread our tarp and were happy to get to bed before dark.

"The next day we were up before daylight and ate our breakfast of sourdough biscuits, hard boiled eggs, coffee and jam. Meals varied but little with exception of substituting fresh side meat for eggs.

"All the way up Garnet Canyon, the peaks loomed high

above, and Jackson Hole Valley seemed to drop into the distance. From here up, we were thankful for ropes and chisels. We chiseled our way step by step; and using the ropes, lassoed projecting ledges.

"When we reached what is called the saddle, we could see into Idaho, the Upper Snake River Valley, and as far as the Twin Buttes near Arco, Idaho. Back and far below was the Jackson Hole Valley, with the shadows of the clouds forming what looked like ink blots on the vast sagebrush floor. We camped at the saddle for another night.

"We arose at 3:30 a.m., ate our breakfast and were on our way up the Grand Teton by 4:00. Bill is a man of little sleep or consideration for the other guy who wants to be in bed past 3 a.m.

"Even though this was August, we were thankful for parkas and gloves. A cold wind was blowing from the glaciers, and snow pockets were all around us. A heavy drifting fog encircled us, and now and then we could see the moon shining through, giving the illusion that it was several times larger than we had ever seen it and traveling a thousand miles a minute. I dreaded to watch it for fear of becoming dizzy. Our hands were numb. I looked at Jack as he stood holding his red nose with his mittened hand while he puffed warm breath into the frosty air. And even though Jack and I felt like complaining once in a while, Billy and Mr. Cooper coaxed us on.

"Several times we tied ropes around all four of us, from one to the other, for more protection. We tried also to set up a slow rhythmic pace for greater safety.

"Climbing the ridge was interesting, as it seemed the mighty rocks were designed to be climbed by some strange method. When we felt we were nearly there and the height was breathtaking, there was still a long way to go.

"Sometime later, we neared the last pitch. Completing this pitch required edging along a crack high above the

Teton glacier, up to what we called 'The Horse's Back' and on to the top of the Grand Teton.

"Here the scenery can be described only by a talented author. We could see more sky than anyone could imaging. The mountains in Idaho and Wyoming were all around us, but none seemed to half equal the majesty of the Grand. The valley below resembled patchwork quilts. The great Snake River—named so perfectly—can be traced from Jackson Lake to Idaho Falls.

"To the east, we saw Jackson Hole and the Wind River Range, to the south the Palisade Range, to the west the Teton Valley, Snake River Valley, Lost River and Sawtooth Ranges. To the north, we could see Island Park and Yellowstone Lake.

"We neatly chiseled our names in the rocks on top, made a little rock monument, then put up a copper flag about twelve by fourteen inches. We also left a bottle with our names inside."

Here, Mr. Petersen hesitated a moment.

"Go on Frank," Daddy said. "I can hardly wait to hear the end to see if you made it back alive, but first tell us how much room there is on top of the peak and what the elevation is there.

"The elevation is 13,766 feet. The top of the peak isn't flat, but jagged and rough, and we measured it fourteen, times twenty seven feet."

"Did you get any pictures of the top?" Daddy asked.

"Yes," replied Mr. Petersen, "and all along the way. I invite you to see them anytime. Rena has them pasted in a scrapbook."

"Yes, and I'm very proud of that scrapbook too," Mrs. Petersen said.

"Now go on and I'll not interfere any more," Daddy said.

"That's quite all right, Jim. I'm glad to explain any

questions which may arise," Mr. Petersen assured him.

"Descending was quite different from ascending. It's far more frightening to go down than up and even more dangerous." Then, laughing and brushing his hand over his mouth and giving his sandy colored mustache a twitch with his upper lip, he went on. "If you slip a bit while climbing you still keep your eyes turned skyward and hope you fall up, but when you go down hill and you slip, all you can see is the very bottom.

"Once Jack's foot went out from under him. He grabbed for me and I grabbed for Billy, but Billy held us firmly with the rope he had fastened securely to a ledge. We followed our same trail and were glad we had chiseled out a few steps and hand holds along the way up. We took one step at a time and securely planted ourselves before we moved the other foot.

"Several times we came to ledges as large as one hundred twenty feet, which we had to scale with ropes."

"Do you consider this climb the most dangerous thing you will ever attempt, Frank?" Mama asked.

"Now that I look back on it, yes, but at the time I thought it was a thrill," Mr. Petersen answered.

"Did you do it for the thrill or the honor and recognition?" asked Daddy.

"I don't know that it ever entered any of our minds to become famous," he answered, "but we did hope to achieve something no man had ever accomplished before. I will have to admit we were all thankful to reach level land. You know children, these peaks were first called 'Pilot Knobs,' because they were noted landmarks for Indians and early mountain trappers."

"What year did you say that was, Frank?" Daddy asked.

"It was in 1898, and several people have climbed it since. My brother-in-law, George Dewey, his sons Jesse, Joseph, and John, accompanied by Nean Christensen from

Teton Valley in Idaho climbed to the top of the Grand a few years later.

"Yes, climbing the Grand Teton is an experience I shall never forget. An experience of rare beauty and great height. An experience given only by God, the Creator of the Great Teton Range."

Owen, Shives and Petersen on top of the Grand Teton. (Picture taken by Mr. Cooper.)

Chapter VII
A RIDE OVER TETON PASS

Mama stood at the kitchen window watching for Daddy to come from town. It seemed it had been a long time, when it actually had been only six hours since he left. She knew he had a lot of business to attend to and consoled herself with that thought, but nevertheless, she showed a release from worry when he came in sight.

He drove to the barn, unhooked the team, watered and fed them, and didn't seem half so anxious to see Mama and us girls as we were to see him.

He hung his overcoat up, kissed Mama and each of us and started telling Mama the news from town.

"A new school marm is the talk of the town today. Seems as though one of the teachers got sick, so this one came in to take her place. The postmaster said she hails from Montana and is very beautiful, about twenty-three years old and single."

"Well, said Mama, "maybe one of these bachelors around here will get his eyes on her, and she will never return to Montana to live. It happened to Olivette Webb, you know. Wonder if we could arrange some way to get her introduced to Bill McInelly?" Then Mama laughed. "Oh, I nearly forgot; you have a letter." Daddy went to his overcoat and pulled a crumpled letter from its pocket.

"Why, it's from father!" she exclaimed, as she took it from Daddy. "Great day! I haven't had a personal letter from him since I was married." She tore the end of the envelope open with shaking hands.

"Dear daughter," she read, "this will come as a surprise to you, coming from me, but your ma is too sick to write. Afraid she is going to have to have an operation for something. The doctor isn't quite sure what is wrong, but she has a lump in her side, and he thinks it is serious."

Mama started to cry. Daddy took the letter from her and read on.

"Don't worry, honey. I'll keep you posted. So far, we haven't had much snow here in Victor, but the old timers are predicting a hard winter. How are Jim and the kids? We hope you are all well. Your mother still worries over you being so far away. Love, Father."

"Well—I'll be," said Daddy, as he dropped the letter on the table.

"Oh, Jim," Mama sniffled, "do you suppose—?" She stopped there and went to the window. "It is such a long way over that Teton Pass into Idaho, but Mother must be awfully sick, or she would have written that letter."

"Well, tomorrow I'll just have to take you and the kids to town and put you on the stage, that's all."

"Can't you get Bill to milk the cow and go with us—just in case?" Mama pleaded.

Daddy hardly knew what to do. He had an irresistible urge to go, yet an indescribable desire to stay. "I hate to turn you loose with the girls all alone, but—" He went to the door, opened it and stood in the doorway looking and listening. "Sounds like a high wind coming up. Maybe by morning there will be a blizzard."

Removing some groceries from a pasteboard box that Daddy had brought from town, Mama went to the bedroom and took some neatly folded socks, underwear and night-gowns and placed them in the box. "I'll pack a few things tonight," she said, "and see what tomorrow brings."

"How far is Idaho, Mama?" I asked.

"A long, long way, my dear," she replied. "So far away it will take us two or three days to get there."

"It is about thirty-seven miles," Daddy said, "and in the wintertime it is three times as far as it is in the summer."

"How much will it cost to ride on the stage?" was Margaret's question.

"More than we can afford," Daddy answered.

The next morning, Margaret awakened before I did. "Are we going Mama? I heard her ask.

"Going where?" I wondered, then remembered "Idaho—Grandma," and sprang to my feet, rubbing the sleep from my eyes.

"We are going to try it if Mr. McInelly will milk old Boss. Daddy has gone to see him now."

Mama went to the cupboard and emptied Rainy Day, the sugar bowl, in which she kept all her spare change. She counted it, and I heard her mutter to herself, "seven dollars and sixty cents. Wonder if that will pay the fare."

"Three days to go and three to come. That's a long time to be gone," I thought. I had never before spent one night away from home since Mama brought me from the Curtis'. I was so excited as Daddy tucked us in Sleigh-Bob with quilts and hot rocks.

The journey to town seemed like the fastest one we had ever taken. Mama had packed a lunch box full of sandwiches, which we ate just before we got to town. Daddy took us to the hotel from where the stage would leave.

"We'll pull out in twenty minutes," the driver told us.

Daddy took the horses to the livery stable and told the man there to keep them until we returned.

We were taken into the hotel, where Mama said we could find a restroom. I was so surprised when we opened the door. It wasn't at all like I expected. I thought it would have a bed and some easy chairs in which to rest. Instead, I found a thing with water in it, and a handle on the side to make the water run. Nevertheless, we felt quite rested by the time we were comfortably transferred from Sleigh-Bob to the stage sleigh, which was pulled by four head of horses. The ride the rest of the day I thought would never end. The road was narrow and sideling, which made it difficult for the horses to keep the sleigh on the road and in the tracks. When

I saw the sleigh box down on one side and up on the other, I clung to Mama.

"All is well," she assured us. "The driver knows how to handle the horses."

He was a large man, stately and kind. His hair was light brown, with a suggestion of gray. He wore a scar on his face from each corner of his mouth down past his chin, which showed signs of his suffering sometime in his life. He spoke kind words to the horses and they obeyed every command.

We were nearing Snake River now and could see the steam rising from the water as it was warmer than the air. The river, partly frozen, yet not hard enough to hold the horses and sleigh, made it difficult for the man running the ferry boat to get us across. Great chunks of slushy ice floated down with the water.

Snake River silently changes its complexion during various seasons. Before we approached it, Mr. Scott, the driver of the stage, told us he expected to find it all creamy-white this morning. He said the day before when he crossed it, it was freezing slushy and today he expected it to be even more frosty.

Then Daddy said, "Yep! This old river is about the most changeable thing I know, except my wife."

Both men laughed, but Mama looked at Daddy with an expression which told him she didn't like that remark, so he went on about the river.

"I have seen it in the spring of the year so high and muddy and foaming with froth, it overflowed its banks. In the late summer and fall, it is often shallow and tame enough for a man to wade. I have seen it dotted with wild Mallard ducks and the banks white with gulls. I have seen it frozen over so solid and covered with snow you would never know there was a river there."

"Yes, I have seen it in all kinds of shapes and colors too, Jim, and I often think whoever named it the 'Snake River' surely picked the right name as its course winds so crooked, yet travels so fast," said Mr. Scott.

As we approached it, we could see a man start the motor, and as it putt-putted we noticed the water began to churn great white waves around the boat, which supported the ferry.

Mama moved over close to us as the horses walked upon the ferry. She expected them to be afraid of it and perhaps refuse to go aboard, then remembered they were used to it as they crossed it every day.

That night, we only made it as far as the Davis Road House, a few miles beyond a little town called Wilson. A man came out to help the stage driver and Daddy take care of the horses. A lady there had a turkey supper all cooked. Such a change from elk meat, it tasted so good to all of us. Her place was very clean, with a pretty winding stairway which led to bedrooms where she gave us soft featherbeds, but her Road House wasn't as nice as the hotel, because it lacked the restroom and running water.

The next morning we were up early. We dressed in such a hurry, because Mama said the lady had breakfast waiting, and the men had gone to hook up the horses. I couldn't find the button hook to button my shoes. I had to go to the table with my shoes unbuttoned. This worried me for fear that the lady would think I wasn't neat. I couldn't enjoy my breakfast thinking about my shoes. Mama looked everywhere, but no button hook could be found. She asked the lady if she could borrow hers, but she didn't have one. The driver and Daddy pulled up to the porch and I started to cry.

"Goodness sakes, Bertha, don't cry or your face will freeze that way," Mama said. "Come here!" Pulling a big metal hairpin from her hair, she buttoned my shoes.

Mr. Scott was the same driver, but he had four different head of horses. He explained to us he used fresh horses which were waiting in the barn at every Road House. This time we had a covered sleigh with a stove on the inside. We were thankful for that as the air was so crisp we could see our breaths. The cover on the sleigh looked just like Daddy's canvas dams. There was a hole in the front end, which we crawled through, and also this hole was used by Mr. Scott to drive the teams.

We were climbing uphill. I could tell by the way the back end of the sleigh tipped down and the front end tipped up. We came to a place Mr. Scott called the Twin Slides and said this was one of the dangerous places on the road in the wintertime when snow slides were running. Shortly beyond this we met a couple of men coming down the hill in a sleigh. They pulled over to the side of the road as far as they could. Mr. Scott also pulled over as far as possible and there wasn't room to pass without shoving the other team off the grade.

"Wait a minute and I'll back up," said our driver. This was a frightening experience to us, but Mr. Scott was familiar with such situations, and the horses were so well trained they put the sleigh right down close to the bank. We couldn't fall off the road as we were against the side of the hill, but each time the sleigh tipped sideling, I got so excited I wanted to jump. I wished I could find a peek hole in the canvas somewhere so I could see out, but the only hole I could see, the driver was using.

We got around each other and started on. After going only a short distance, we reached the top of the summit where we stopped at another Road House for dinner. It was a much smaller place than the first Road House, and other than for a barn, it was the only building in sight. When the driver went in to dinner, he kissed the cook. She and her pretty teen-age daughter, Evelyn, were there alone.

After we ate dinner, Daddy and Mr. Scott changed horses again. Mr. Scott knew each horse, and I couldn't figure out how he could remember each one's name. We kept the same sleigh. The cook gave the driver an order for groceries that he would bring back to her the next day. He threw a kiss to the cook and the girl as we departed and said, "She is the best wife a man ever had. Not many women would stay there and work like that in such a lonely place. It isn't bad now, but in the dead of the winter she is isolated there alone when I can't get through the drifts, sometimes for days. Our daughter goes to school in Victor and goes up with me over weekends and holidays.

About three o'clock that afternoon, we passed a place Mr. Scott called Windy Gulch and said, "This is another dangerous place when slides are running."

I felt relieved when we passed that place. The wind blowing and whistling through the trees caused little bunches of crusted snow to drop from the branches. Mr. Scott let us take turns sticking our heads out the hole to see the wintry sights. We could see the road drifting full of snow in places. Once he handed the lines to Daddy, and he climbed out and walked ahead to measure the depth of the next drift.

"It's all right," he said as he climbed back in the sleigh.

The sun had dropped over the west mountains ahead of us before we reached the Road House at the bottom of the mountain. The barn sat on one side of the road and a big Road House on the other. This place, the largest and best of any, looked mighty good to us, but still no running water. Mr. Bircher came from the house to help with the teams. There we met a family consisting of a man and wife and five children who were headed for Jackson. This Road House was big enough to accommodate many people. The barn was big enough to hold about sixteen head of horses.

Mrs. Bircher lit a lantern and hung it on a hook from the ceiling, then lit a kerosene light and put it on the table. She had baked ham for supper. She asked Mama if we wanted one bedroom or two. Mama said one would be fine. We were taken to a bedroom on the main floor. The room was covered with a rag carpet. Mama complimented the lady about the pretty rug. She said she enjoyed making rag rugs to pass away long wintry days. Also in our room we found a big white-china wash basin and a pitcher full of water; clean towels hung on a rack, and a kerosene light was on the dresser. This gave us a new feeling of comfort. The rest of the guests were taken upstairs, where they occupied two rooms.

After breakfast, the men came to the house with four different horses, but still the same sleigh. We crossed the Wyoming-Idaho state line about two hours later. At one o'clock we reached Victor. The stage stopped at the post office there and unloaded the mail, and Mr. Scott said he would take us to Grandpa's farm. They lived about two and a half miles further.

Even though Grandma was very sick in bed, a smile came over her face, and she cried when she saw us.

"What a happy surprise this is," she said, as Mama bent over her bed and kissed her.

"Ho, ho! You did come in answer to my letter, didn't you darling?" Grandpa said, as he took Mama in his arms. He was a tall, thin, raw-boned person, with blonde curly hair, a mustache, and removable teeth.

Then Mama sat on the edge of Grandma's bed and held her hand. Grandma looked so tiny and thin lying in that bed. Mama asked all sorts of questions about Grandma's health, then reached to a little stand nearby and got a hairbrush and fixed Grandma's hair all pretty.

This was a little house they lived in—only three rooms with the bare logs showing from within. As I could only see one bed, I began to wonder where we were going to sleep, when in came Mama's sister, Aunt Lula Kearsley. She lived close to Grandma and had come to see how she felt. Of course, she was surprised to see us, and invited us to her house. It was the largest home I had ever been in. A kind and patient uncle and so many cousins lived there, I got con-

70

fused. There were eight cousins and I heard Mama ask her sister that night if she hoped for a boy or a girl this time.

Upon being ready to retire to bed, Mama said, "Come here Bertha!" She held my Tom-Thumbs in her hand. She slipped one on each thumb, for without them I sucked my thumbs all night. The next morning, one of my handsome teen-age boy cousins teased me about my Tom-Thumbs. They came off right then, never to be put on again.

We went to the barn with our cousins to milk a whole herd of cows, feed a hundred sheep or more, and to feed turkeys and geese. They told us they would soon have so many new lambs they would be running all over the place.

While we were there, a terrible blizzard moved in. Uncle Ed came home from town and said the Teton Pass would be closed tomorrow.

Grandma improved slowly and my folks were getting anxious to get home, but for three days and nights the wind blew and snow whirled so hard we couldn't see the fence around the yard. Three feet of new snow fell in those three days, drifts piled high, and we couldn't even get to town. We didn't mind; we were enjoying our first adventure so far away from home. Besides that, our cousins couldn't get to school so we played games at their house while Mama visited and helped care for Grandma.

Finally, on our way home again, we stopped at the same Road House at the bottom of the hill the first night. We had six head of horses this time as the roads were drifted full. About four o'clock, we reached there hungry and tired, for we hadn't had anything to eat since we left our aunt's home. Too late to go on, we stayed there that night.

The second day we were up and eating breakfast before daybreak. As soon as day dawned, we were on our way, but didn't see the sun until we nearly reached the top of the mountain, for we were on the shady side.

About the time we reached the place they called "The

71

Switch Backs," the horses were wallowing snow to their bellies. The driver knew how to lay the reins to the horses so they slapped each horse at the same time, causing them to plunge from their tracks to make some new ones. Once they were in snow nearly over their backs. Their tracks blew full behind us. Daddy and Mr. Scott were in and out of the sleigh many times to shovel snow and help the horses, but not once did Mr. Scott speak an unkind word to his teams. Every time the horses plunged, Erma cried. Mama had to keep reassuring us everything was fine.

The cook, glad to see the driver that night, said she had really been lonely those three long, blizzardy days.

The next day, we had the sunny side of the slope and made much better time going downhill. We had to break road all the way though, because no other outfit had traveled the road since the storm. People figured where the mail sleigh couldn't go, neither could they.

We got to the Road House at the bottom of the mountain at one p.m. There, we had dinner and were on our way again. Mr. Scott said he knew everyone would be anxious for the mail that day.

Getting Dan and Bally at four p.m., we were on our last stretch home, but didn't arrive there until midnight, as the roads were drifted full from town to our house.

The house was cold, but Daddy soon had two fires going. Mama heated some flat irons on the stove, wrapped them in blankets, tucked us in bed with them at our feet, then took a deep sigh and said, "What a nice visit we had. I think I can be contented here on Poverty Flats for a few more years."

Chapter VIII
THE WEDDING PARTY

Just before school let out for summer vacation, Flora Babstead greeted the world gladly and announced her wedding date.

A young man by the name of Barney Raymond had come from Montana, claiming to be a good ranch hand. Mr. Babstead hired him. Barney had curly, blonde hair, a perfect build, a height of six feet, a whimsical sense of humor, and a soothing voice. Flora had just turned seventeen, and Barney twenty four. He promised her diamond rings, furs, bright lights and entertainment in social places. Flora's provincial upbringing and restricted life hardly prepared her for such a change.

Torn between two loves, one for the quiet, extraordinary beauty of her flat Creek home, the other for this unpredictable character who had suddenly swooped into her life, Flora found herself completely frustrated.

Barnabus, as he liked to be called, confessed to her one evening, while they were sitting on the top rail of the buck fence in front of her house, that his chief occupation wasn't ranching, but making marriage plans with a beautiful girl.

"What is your occupation, your ambition, and desire in life," Flora asked very hesitatingly.

"Well, I once started to study to become an interior decorator," he said, then paused — "but somehow, I got the roaming blood in me, and I wanted to see the world. I really think I have been searching for you," he continued, as he jumped from the fence and pulled her with him. Then after pulling her face close to his and kissing her lips, said, "but what does it matter, so long as we have each other?" Then holding her at arm's length from him, he admired her golden hair, flying in the moonlight, and said, "Only by living with me will you ever know completely what happiness there is

73

in this world."

In less than three weeks, they were married.

At five o'clock, the late afternoon sunlight had turned the delicate hues of the blue crusted snow on the mountain tops, to a glorious golden haze. The sun was sinking behind the Teton Range, and daylight was fading fast when Judge Boucher performed the wedding in the Babstead home. That evening, a dance was held in the Flat Creek Schoolhouse. The desks were carried outside. The little schoolhouse's personality completely changed. Gas lanterns hung all around the room, and the place smelled fragrant with wild flowers, giving it charm and elegance.

This being the first dance I had ever attended, and Flora the first bride I had ever seen, made me so curious, I had a hard time restraining myself enough to keep out of the wedding march. I would have been the first in line behind the bride and groom as they entered the door of the schoolhouse to the music of the piano had Mama not pulled me back several times.

Flora looked radiant and glamourous that night, and played a natural role as if she had rehearsed being a bride before. Mrs. Babstead made her wedding gown of white crepe-de-Chine, with long sleeves, and underneath, Flora wore a white satin petticoat. Her gown was held together in the back with tiny, covered buttons, from the neck past the waist line. The skirt touched the floor. She wore a strand of pearls around her neck and glittery combs in her hair. White frosting and pink roses decorated her three tiered wedding cake.

The piano was rented from the Town Hall. Daddy and Mr. Babstead moved it to the schoolhouse. Our teacher played the piano while Mr. Kelly strummed the guitar. The honored couple danced to the wedding march, then every couple present joined in dancing a waltz. Before long, someone suggested a Virginia Reel. Mr. Van Leerdam pulled a harmonica from his vest pocket and the musicians played "Turkey in the Straw."

There were only two chairs in the building, and the musicians occupied them, so everyone had to keep dancing. The Virginia Reel was hard on the fat women. They puffed and panted until their husbands felt sorry for them and carried some blocks of wood in for them to sit on. The music went on, but about three tunes were played before the women had breath enough to dance.

The bride and groom received many useful gifts. Someone gave them a washtub and scrubbing board. Another couple gave them a rolling pin with some cooking utensils. They received towels, a looking glass, a dishpan, a water bucket and drinking dipper, three flat irons with one tranferrable handle, a milk strainer, four bars of homemade lye soap, and, for a joke, someone gave them a hot water bottle with a note attached telling Flora it would be a good bed partner to keep her feet warm.

There were more children present at this dance than there ever were at the Flat Creek picnics. We sat on the floor in one corner and many times we thought some big peson might step or fall on us. About ten o'clock, there were some sleepy little ones. The teacher suggested we use her curtained off corner and all the children could go to bed. The infants, six of them, were already on her bed, so our parents took some coats and put them down on the floor, took our shoes off, laid us on the coats and covered us with left-over wraps.

Bob Seaton, young Ben Goe, and Charlie Petersen were neither old enough to dance nor young enough to be put to bed. They were the ones who did the devilment. They took buggy seats out of the groom's buggy, hid them, tied tin cans filled with rocks to long wires, and fastened them to the back of the buggy.

I awoke several times. The same noise of music and

chatter filled the schoolroom. I tried pulling a coat up over my head to help smother the sound, but then my feet stuck out. I thought, "What a task to try to sleep in this condition with snoring kids on either side of me."

When I raised up, Louise Goe whispered, "Are you awake?"

I answered her, "Yes, and I'm getting up."

She said, "I'll join you."

We crawled out of our warm spots, put our shoes on, but couldn't button them. I went to Mama and whispered, "I want to stay up." She took a hairpin from her hair and buttoned my shoes, then buttoned Louise's.

Elmer Moody pulled his watch from his vest pocket and announced, "It is midnight and I suggest the happy couple come forward to make a speech and cut the wedding cake."

Flora and Barnabus walked across the floor, holding hands. Mr. Moody said, "I knew only one couple would come forward when I said, 'the HAPPY couple.' Speech, speech!" Everyone laughed and clapped.

Mr. Babstead carried the punch in from outside. Mrs. Babstead served while Flora served the wedding cake.

"Now, said Mr. Kelly, "I think I'm good for a few more hours." And everyone else felt the same way.

About two a.m., Louise and I pulled our shoes off and went back to our place among the kids, but that place wasn't there. We went around the pile of cloaks serveral time trying to find a hole in which to crawl. We decided to get in someway. We took a man's big coat right off the top, rolled ourselves in it, snuggled up against the rest and soon were asleep again.

"I surely did enjoy that dance, Jim," I heard Mama say on our way home early the next morning. "Even if I do have big bags under my eyes and blistered feet, I'm glad we went. I don't think there'll be another dance like that one for a long time."

Chapter IX
THE RAMPAGING GROS VENTRE

Margaret awakened one morning shouting, "Today's my birthday, today's my birthday!"

A birthday was always treated as a special occasion at our house, and the one belonging to it had the honor of being "Queen" or "King" for that day. This was a promise which was fulfilled by Mama. Daddy never had time to be worried with such trifling matters as birthdays, but he was a thoughtful Daddy, so after breakfast he hooked Dan and Bally to Lumber Wagon, making ready to take us to school. It had been raining steadily for three weeks, causing the ground to be so muddy we couldn't walk. Dark clouds and high winds told Daddy the storm still wasn't over, but he felt an ambitious streak, and all this storm had made him anxious to get his crops planted. He drove to the house and asked Mama if she would like to go with him to Grovont to buy some seed grain from his brother.

"This is the last day of school," said Mama. "Why not wait until tomorrow and we can take the girls with us? Besides this, it is Margaret's birthday and I promised her a cake."

"I can't wait," Daddy said. "I am already a week late in getting my crops planted. This is the eighteenth day of May, but if you can't go I'll take the girls to school and go from there."

Though Mama enjoyed being a homebody, she never turned down a chance to go anywhere. She turned to Margaret and said, "Honey, I'll take your new dress with me and work on it on the way and then make your cake after I get home, and we will have it for supper tonight, then when we finish eating, each of you girls may recite your recitations to us which you are to give on the program today. Is that all right?"

When we reached the schoolhouse, we coaxed Mama to let Archie stay with us. We thought it would be fun to show little brother off during the day. The teacher gave her permission, as we were having a party and celebrating the last day of school, but Archie cried to go with Daddy. Mama kissed each of us when we jumped from Lumber Wagon and said they would be back in time to pick us up that afternoon from school. We waved and threw kisses until they were out of sight.

"I hate to leave the girls like this, and especially on one of their birthday anniversaries, but it gives them courage and will help them to live even one day at a time better, knowing plans must be changed once in a while," Mama said, as she rearranged Earl on her lap and put her arm around Archie who sat on the seat beside her.

When they crossed the Gros Ventre River bridge, Daddy said to Mama, "Look at the water Berla, it is muddy and high. This rain we have had is the cause of this. Funny we haven't had floods. And look at that big cloud above us. We may get wet before we get home."

At the other end of the bridge sat a man on horseback, very alert, with a pair of binoculars to his eyes. As they approached him, Daddy stopped the team to talk with him. He lived neighbors to Uncle Andy. He said, "I'm watching this bridge, and the water above it. We are a little fearful this high water may wash the bridge out. I guess you've heard what is happening?"

"No," answered Daddy, but I can see the river is high."

"The dam at the Gros Ventre slide is spilling over. All this rain we have had melted the snow so fast it caused the lake to fill to overflowing," the man on the horse said.

This huge dam had been formed two years prior to this time, when the side of a mountain gave away at the top, causing a huge earth and rock slide. This was the place where Daddy and Mr. Goe had seen the big crevasse when

78

they crossed it with webs. The slide being approximately one and a half miles long, a half mile wide, and several hundred feet deep, took less than two minutes to run entirely across the valley, blocking off the Gros Ventre River and forming the tremendous dam, which blocked the canyon.

"We hired some engineers to look the dam over yesterday, and they pronounced it safe. They were sure it would hold, but it is spilling over now," said the neighbor.

"Oh, dear! Jim. Let's go back right now. The bridge may go out," coaxed Mama.

"This bridge won't go today," said Daddy, "that is, before we get back." With these words, he laid the reins to the horses' backs and jokingly said to the man, "Keep a good eye on it and don't let it go out until we get back in about two hours."

As they rode up to Uncle Andy's house, he was mounting his horse, ready to leave. "I didn't expect to see you today, Jim. Don't you know the dam is breaking loose? The pressure of the water storming over the dam is causing the south end of it to crumble. I'm now on my way to warn the people living below the dam to evacuate their homes. This is serious and I must hurry. Take the kids and Berla and go on in and visit with Ida. I'll be back sometime today."

"I just came for a few sacks of seed grain and if you don't mind, I'll help myself and be on my way," said Daddy.

"Yes, help yourself," said Uncle Andy as he kicked his horse in its flanks.

"Let's go home now, Jim! We have children waiting for us," Mama pleaded.

Just then, another man rode up on a horse and shouted, "You are too late! The bridge is gone. I saw a wall of water coming, then a man floating on a hayrack and I had to run my horse to higher grounds for safety. The dam has broken and released the lake."

Daddy, Mama, Uncle Andy, Aunt Ida, and many others

79

rushed toward the river, but stopped on a hill by the little church where they could witness the tragedy which was happening. For many, a losing battle was taking place against treacherous, rampaging muddy waters, demanding respect. A little town which consisted of a blacksmith shop, a sawmill, a store and flour mill, a garage, a taxidermist shop, twenty seven homes, and many farm buildings, were carried down with the flood waters like match boxes. All that remained of the little community of Kelly were the schoolhouse and churchhouse which stood on higher land.

Six persons lost their lives. Among them were Aunt Ida's father, stepmother, and little half brother; the Kneedy family who lived close to the bank of the river. They tried to escape, but were too late. Others were Mama's cousin, Clint Stevens, a man twenty two years old, who when last seen alive, was riding on the roof of a chicken coop. Two ladies, Mrs. Lovejoy and her sister, both quite elderly who lived alone, heeded the warning and after harnessing their team, stopped at their house to load some valuables. They saw the wall of water coming, and climbed to their buggy when the waves engulfed them. One was driving and the other one lashing the lines to the horses. What a gruesome sight for those who witnessed this treacherous flood as it churned along, leaving only greasy, clay banks.

When the mean, snarling water subsided, four of the bodies were recovered the first day. Some men found Mama's cousin the following day, and the body of one of the sisters was never found. The five bodies were taken to the little church near my uncle's home, where Daddy, Mama and many others worked on them for two days, pumping their lifeless limbs to release the water from their bodies. The women sewed burial clothes while the men built caskets. They were given services in the little church and all laid to rest in the same cemetery.

On the afternoon of the flood, about three o'clock, a man

riding a horse brought word of the disaster to our little school. So excited and confused he could hardly talk, he told us girls our parents and two brothers were victims of the flood. Our teacher put her arms around us and held us close to her, saying she felt sure that the report wasn't true. We stood there crying when Mr. Goe came. He offered to take us to his house, but we wanted to go home. He drove us there and asked if we felt safe to stay alone.

I lit the fire in the kitchen stove. Margaret made some toast and cocoa. It didn't taste like the toast and cocoa Mama made, and when I tried to swallow, my throat nearly refused to let the food down.

Mr. McInelly heard about our plight and came that night to milk Boss. He asked us to go home with him, but we still insisted we wanted to stay on Poverty Flats. We all three got in Mama's and Daddy's bed. After we blew out Carrie, the house was darker than I had ever seen it. Without the sound of the little boys, everything was hushed and quiet. Erma started to cry. That made Margaret feel bad, and she cried, which made me feel bad, and I cried. We got out of bed and knelt beside it and offered a prayer, asking God to please return our parents and brothers to us safely.

The first day was a long lonely one. We fed the chickens, gathered the eggs four times, and tidied up the house. Margaret found a small piece of chalk among her school possessions that she had brought home the day before, and we used it to play games on the back of the kitchen stove, which served us for years as a blackboard. We drank more cocoa, ate more toast, watched the road and cried.

The second day was a repetition of the first. We didn't go anywhere, and we saw no one except Mr. McInelly, who came twice a day to milk Boss. We were still sure there wasn't anything in the house to eat except toast and cocoa.

The third day, we walked to the mailbox to see if there could possibly by any mail. We knew there wouldn't be word from our parents, because the bridge and road were washed out, but we were hoping for a letter from Grandma or someone. What a disappointment to us to find the mailbox empty, but it at least gave us something to do. We took our time returning to the house. We picked wild flowers, took our shoes and stockings off and waded in the ditch.

That day, the water subsided, enabling Daddy to throw a rock, with two notes attached, across the river to a man. One note read, "Will you please deliver this message to my children, or have someone do it, so they will know we are alive?" The other note read, "Dear Children: All four of us are safe at Uncle Andy's but can't get home until the water goes down and the bridge is fixed. We hope someone is staying with you and milking Boss. Don't worry. We love you and will be home soon."

At four o'clock that day, the man rode horseback all the way to our house and personally delivered the note. We recognized Daddy's handwriting. We cried again, this time tears of joy.

The next day, men were able to put a wire cable across the river. They fastened a big, round tin tub to it. Daddy and Archie got in the tub and Daddy got them across the river by pulling hand-over-hand on the cable. He then sent the tub back to the other side, by use of the cable, then Mama and Earl climbed in, and Mama pulled them across. Mr. Walt Spicer sat waiting with his team and buggy on the side of the river where Daddy, Mama and the boys safely landed; and he delivered them home after dark, just after we girls had eaten our thirteenth meal of toast and cocoa.

Gros Ventre flood taken from the Teton Valley Ranch toward Black Tail Butte. May 18, 1927.

Guil Huff sitting on the shores of the lake in Jackson Hole which was formed by the mountain slide.

Chapter X
PASTLES AND CALASES

We had many varieties of entertainment while growing up on our "Poverty Flats." In our back yard stood a formation of slate rocks. Layer upon layer, these rocks arose from the ground. They were covered with an orange, rusty substance and green moss, with pinnacles reaching upwards toward the sky.

We Chambers children were like most other children, in the respect that we too had strong imaginations. Margaret, the one of us who had the biggest imagination, was constructive and creative, and always looking for something new on our place to explore. She was the one who led us to these rocks, and picked a general portion, marked it off and called it "her castle." I chose the next domain, and we bequeathed little Erma the rest, but being quite happy with the small bit we left her, she never complained nor begged for a larger allotment.

One day, Mama read us a story about a prince living in a palace with a beautiful princess. From then on, I wasn't quite sure if those rocks were castles or palaces. In my confusion, I often called them pastles or calases.

Many wild flowers grew close to our "castles." We decorated with sego lilies, rooster heads, buttercups, roses or columbines. We spent hours playing there and dreaming about someday living in a real palace with a real prince. Mama told us we were building air castles, but taught us that many fine and wonderful things could happen to us if we kept our dreams high and searched for the finer things in life.

We visited this land of imagination again and again, always finding something new and exciting. We loved to loiter there in the sun and probe the unfathomable. I planned much of my future life, how I could live it, what kind of home I would live in, how I would search the big universe around me until I found exactly the right prince to live with, how many children we would have, what their names would be, how each of them would grow up to be a perfect prince or princess.

We were drawn with a compulsion to these castles, like a high tension power line on which we had seized hold and could not let go. I felt close to God while playing there, and I wanted to be able to teach my children to feel close to Him, that they too might have high ideals. I wanted to live my life every day like a fairy tale ends: "And they lived happily ever after."

At the base of these rocks, where they ended, the draw began with its own peculiar personality. In this draw, we saw many interesting and awe-inspiring things each day. We learned how birds soar. We watched them glide and fly around looking for prey. When a large bird such as a raven, hawk or eagle could spot a baby rabbit, a squirrel, a mouse, a chicken or any other small animal, it would fly above the smaller animal, charming or hypnotizing it, then it would pounce upon its prey, sink its long talons into the flesh and numb the animal until death overtook the creature.

We learned how these birds build nests. We watched hundreds of little mud swallows build nests in the cliffs. These we called "Cliff Dwellers." The large birds, including eagles, built their nests in the tops of the tallest trees to be found. They made them of twigs, pineboughs or whatever they found available.

My imagination really soared whenever I was in that draw, especially when we passed the shadowy caverns. Daddy showed us a place where one time he wanted to test a stick of dynamite to see how powerful it was. He had an old blue teakettle he placed on the ground, then put the dynamite under it, and lit the fuse. This is the story he told us:

"It blew the teakettle in the sky so far it never came down."

I continued looking for that teakettle in the draw, either on the ground where it should have finally made its way back to earth after many years, or in the sky where I expected to find it suspended. When I first heard about the big dipper in the sky, I thought someone had gotten all mixed up and called it a big dipper when it really was a teakettle.

Always we were most delighted when the Goe children would come to see us, and especially when they brought two or three horses. We piled three and four deep on Topsy, Ginger and Champ to go back in the draw to pick wild gooseberries or currants. Florence always reminded us to be careful not to bang the buckets together, for this scared the horses and they would jump sideways and pile us. We organized ourselves into two groups, seeing which side could pick the most berries.

All alone one day picking service berries, Louise and I were both up high in a big bush. This day we climbed the mountain, taking a long time to go around each briar and sticker to avoid scratching our legs. With our buckets and tummies about half-full of most delicious berries, our mouths had a smear of juice all around them, and we were laughing at the sight of each other when a mad mother wolf let us know we were trespassing close to her den where she had her whelps hidden. As she let out a vociferous cry, her whelps began to yelp in unison, and they sounded as though they were directly under us. We fell out of the bush on our backs, but managed to hang on to our buckets. It took us thirteen minutes to get back home, the same distance it had taken fifty minutes to climb. We had about seven or eight berries apiece in our buckets when we stopped running.

After the berry season ended, we found another project. We gathered pine-gum. Some would be hard, and some so soft it stuck to our teeth, causing everything we ate for days to taste like pitch. Being very careful, we soon learned how to mix the hard with the soft so it masticated to a most pleasant consistency. Margaret taught us how to mold it with our fingers into squares, and place each piece on the outside of the window sill to dry in the sun. When the Goe children came to play, we sold them a square of gum for a penny. One day, Bill and Byron asked us how we molded gum to go into such perfect squares. We were smart enough to know if we told them we chewed it first, they wouldn't buy any more.

There were owls of nearly every specie in that draw, and they could make the most weird screeches and hoots. Even in broad daylight, they could turn me around and head me back in the same direction from which I had just come. One day, I was alone in the draw. Mama had sent me for Old Boss. Usually one of my sisters and I went together, but this time Mama wanted them to do another task, so she put her hand on my shoulder and said, "Go cheerfully along, my dear, and all will be well."

Daddy had told Mama he would be working at the beaver ponds that day, tearing them out and building a dam below. He said it would be quite late when he got back, so please have Boss in the barn. Mama said if it was very late, she would have Boss milked when he got home.

I found Boss and we traveled fast through the draw. Daddy always warned us against running the cow, because it would make her milk hot and cause it to spoil easily. I imagined all sorts of crazy, horrible sounds, and decided to run her a little way to hurry her past the most frightening part; then I would slow her down and let her walk on in.

We were about halfway home when a screeching hoot echoed between the walls of the canyon. I turned around and started running in the opposite direction. By then, another owl answered the call from the first one. It came from the direction we were headed. There I stood, paralyzed in my tracks, without much choice to make. It didn't seem to bother Boss. She was headed home. I figured it would be better for me to follow her than to be left alone in the draw surrounded by hooting owls. It was a perfect hide-out for ghosts or headless horsemen who rode by night. I put my feet down hard and fast on terra firma, and Boss and I ran all the rest of the way to the barn.

That night, Mama put Old Boss in the stanchion to milk her. She threw her a forkful of hay so she would stand still while Mama milked. Daddy often milked her right out in the open, but Mama felt safer when she put Boss' head between two bars.

Mama sent me to the house to tend baby brother and to iron a few handkerchiefs and pillow cases she had left before the fire went down and the flat irons cooled off, on the stove. When I finished ironing, I took Archie by the hand and told my sisters to look after baby Earl. We went for a walk to watch Mama milk. While we were watching the warm milk being expressed and land in the foamy mass in the bucket, Old Boss started stepping from side to side.

"Soe, Boss, Soe!" Mama kept talking to her in cow language, but she refused to stand still. Her senses were much keener than Mama's or mine. Mama finally realized there must be danger, or why was Boss trying to get away?

Just then,, a cry came down from the canyon that numbed me. Mama ran to the door of the barn to listen. I grabbed Archie in my arms and Mama said, "That is the cougar your Daddy told me about. He saw his tracks the other day up the creek. Take brother and run for the house."

"What about you Mama? I don't want to leave you here with the cow alone," I protested.

"I'm nearly through milking and I'll be right in," she said.

Old Boss held her milk back and wouldn't let another

drop come. Mama freed her from the stanchion, but closed the door and bolted it, leaving her inside, then went to the house.

Another cry, then another one, came. Each cry sounded to me like a child in distress. Even though the doors of the house were both closed, we could hear the cry from that cat through the walls. Mama explained to us that the cry of a cougar, a panther, or a mountain lion sounded very similar to the cry of a baby. It came closer and closer.

The night grew dark, and still Daddy wasn't home. Mama paced the floor, but once when I mentioned that I would be happy to see Daddy safely home, Mama comforted me with, "Daddy can take care of himself. He could turn that cougar wrong side out with his bare fists and head him the other way if he got close enough to him." She put Copper Topper on the stove and said, "Sing, teakettle, sing. That will bring father home." She explained to us that was an old English custom and saying.

Mama's facial expression changed when she heard Daddy's whistle that night.

The next spring I heard Daddy and Mama discussing Old Boss. "Her milk is so weedy I'm afraid to give it to the children for fear of making them sick," Mama said. "Why don't you do something about it, Jim?"

"Now, Berla, I can't pen the cow up, nor can I chew her food. Milk is always weedy in the spring. You know that. Be patient and I'll dry her up in a few days," Daddy said.

Mama knew this meant we would be without milk for a long time, perhaps a month or more. "Weedy milk is better than none," she said, "and it isn't easy to feed children without milk."

They kept one of Boss's calves and named her Curley, but Mama knew it would be several months before Curley had a calf. Daddy told her that he had been talking with Mr. Winegar and he had an extra cow their family didn't need so he would lend the cow to us and take Old Boss and Curley to the range with his dry stock. Daddy agreed to pay Mr. Winegar in the fall with so many bushels of wheat for the use of his cow and the pasture for Boss and Curley.

One day, Mama and we children were all alone in the house when we saw a man coming on horseback. Mr. Winegar rode up and Mama stepped out in the yard to greet him. He very humbly and softly broke the news to Mama that he had been riding on the range checking on the cattle and he found where a bear had killed Old Boss.

The tears rolled down Mama's face, because she loved that cow next to Daddy and us children more than anything on the ranch, including Dan and Bally.

Mama remembered then the time when the butcher rode up to our place hoping Daddy had a beef to sell. Daddy knew he could worry Mama a bit so he said, "No, Butch, I don't have a beef to sell, but there's Old Boss. She's kinda old and stiff in her hind parts, but I might as well sell her to you for meat or she'll die someday anyway."

"It's all right with me, sir Hon, if you sell the cow," Mama said, "but I get to set the price on her."

The author, sitting on her "Castle" years later.

Chapter XI
FRITZ YELLOWHAIR

After putting up hay most of the day, Daddy came in from the field with sweat pouring off his face. It was a hot summer day in August, and he carried the scent of sweet clover with him. We children and Mama were in the house, where it was cooler than outside in the scorching sun.

Wiping his forehead with his red bandana handkerchief, he leaned to brace himself against the door frame and said, "Guess what?"

"You've finished the haying," Mama said.

"Company is coming," I guessed as I ran to the window with disappointment.

"You caught another live rabbit," Erma said.

"You are all wrong," replied Daddy, as he stepped over the threshold. "I just came to the house for a cool drink of lemonade and discovered we have a dog."

"A dog?," we all shouted in unison. We ran to the door to see. Daddy loved to pull jokes on us, and we weren't sure that this might be a joke.

"See for yourselves," Daddy said, as he followed us outside. "I saw him yesterday in the Indian camp at the mouth of the draw. The Indians got that far day before yesterday and camped. I saw them shooting rockchucks with a .22 gun."

"What were they shooting rockchucks for?" asked Margaret.

"They do this in the summer and dry the meat for their winter food," answered Daddy. "This morning, I saw them moving north, and this dog was following them, but limping."

"Oh dear," I said. "He will never catch up now. How far do you think they have gone without him Daddy?"

"I don't know, but we will probably never see them

again."

We went out to see how friendly or fierce he may be. He was lying in the shade under Lumber Wagon. We coaxed him, whistled at him, tried feeding him, but he just laid there with his chin resting on his front paws, frightened at all of us and refused to move. We started calling him all the dog names we could think of, but realized none of them would fit him, for he, being an Indian dog, had to have an Indian name. Mama suggested we call him Fritz Yellowhair.

When Daddy examined Fritz Yellowhair, he discovered the cushions of his feet were worn down to the quick. He had traveled so many miles he could go no further.

"No wonder this dog is lame. If he could only speak," Daddy said, "I'll bet he could tell us a lot."

We fed him and made him a comfortable bed of straw in a large box, but he refused to own it. He much preferred lying under Lumber Wagon.

It took us quite a while to understand Fritz. He had a personality all his own. He didn't whine, bark, wag his tail, nor play like any well-trained dog would have. It even took Fritz longer to understand us. We were quite sure he wondered why we lived as we did and not like Indians.

One day, Daddy decided to kill Fritz. He figured if he was going to lie around like a "dodo" he wasn't worth feeding. "One way to judge a good dog is to observe him and see what he is worth," Daddy thought, "and this dog is absolutely worthless."

He didn't tell us anything about his plans, for he knew there would be a lot of tears all over the place. He went to one drawer to get his shells for Meat-in-the-pot, but the box was empty. The next day, Daddy went to town and while there he tried to buy some shells, but the hardware store didn't have a shell to fit his gun. Daddy didn't have any desire to be outright cruel so decided to give the dog a better chance.

Within a few days, Fritz's fright had left him. He began to jump upon us, wag his tail, and plead with us, with droopy eyelids and a special whine, to play with him. We soon taught him how to play hide-and-seek by making him stand by the kitchen door until we were hidden. Then we whistled, and when he found us he barked, jumped, and made a trip back to the house, but refused to stay there long enough for us to hide again, unless we too reported back to the goal and instructed him to do so. Fritz Yellowhair had now changed completely.

Daddy had been paying us children one penny for each squirrel we could kill, and one nickel for each rockchuck, giving us our choice in the way we wished to kill them. Trying traps, poison and water, we found water the quickest.

Carrying tubs full of water to pour down burrows where squirrels or chucks enter is about the slowest recommendation I can make to become rich.

We were sure we had the outlet to the burrows plugged first, then the hard work began. These wise little animals always have at least two burrows for entrances to their home, and sometimes we plugged up to seven.

Taking Fritz with us one day, we taught him the game of "Drowning-out." The minute we started pouring water, Fritz Yellowhair became excited. When the burrow got full of water and the animal could no longer breathe, he had to come out for air, and Fritz Yellowhair, being trigger quick, would grab him and shake him until dead, then lay him at our feet and whine, just as if to say, "Well, pet me a bit; I helped you again."

We could tell Fritz loved this sport, because as soon as he killed one squirrel he would immediately run to another hole, dig and whine. Many times, the dog tangled with a chuck nearly as big as he, but showed no fear of any of them.

We were all in the field helping Daddy haul off rocks one

93

day, when Margaret saw an animal go down a hole. We three girls started begging to be dismissed so we could get our tub. Daddy gave his permission, so we commenced carrying water from an irrigation ditch, which went on for more than an hour. Guarding the hole while we went for more, Fritz stood motionless with his nose to the hole. We were nearly ready to give up, thinking he had outsmarted us and had escaped from another outlet, when, to our surprise, a big badger sprang forth. At first sight, our eyes were dazzled by the hugeness of this animal. The fight was on. Fritz snarled and yelped while the badger frothed and growled. Even though the badger was weak from the water and soaked to his hide, he had more fight in him than Fritz had bargained for. We tried hitting the badger with a club, but about the time he was on top of the wrestling match where we could get in a lick, the tables turned and Fritz rolled up. When we saw blood spurting and couldn't tell from which animal, we screamed for Daddy. He came running with a pitchfork to where we were, looked the situation over and decided he had to help Fritz in order to save his life, but he couldn't get a good stab in either, because dog over badger and badger over dog wouldn't allow him to stab.

At one time during the fight, the animals had each other by the tail. Breathless with excitement, we watched them as they tangled long enough that the badger's fur began to dry out. The growling getting weaker and weaker, Fritz gave up and lay motionless with the life seemingly gone from his body, and the badger nearly as limp.

We girls cried so many tears we thought they would flow in rivers and drown out all the burrowing animals on Flat Creek.

"Now be patient, and persevering!" Daddy soothed us. "We are the onlookers, so we must cheer instead of cry, or Fritz will think we have lost faith in him."

"But, Daddy, if our dog can't fight anymore, the badger

94

may come to and dissect him," cried Margaret.

"Please Daddy, finish killing the badger," Erma pleaded.

"No, he's nearly done for now; let him suffer it out. I'm more concerned what to do for Fritz. I may have to make a stretcher to lift him to Lumber Wagon."

Daddy took his pitchfork and rolled the badger over. This brought a grunt from the dying animal. Fritz heard it and opened his eyes and, to our amazement, sprang to his feet. He had his second wind now. He grabbed ol' badger at the back of the head and shook him so quickly and viciously it broke his neck. After all the life was completely gone from the badger's body, Fritz stood on him with his front paws sunk deep into his fur, his nose pointed toward the sky and yelped in little 'yip yips,' claiming his victory.

Mama laid Fritz Yellowhair on the kitchen floor, bathed his wounds in epsom salts, wrapped his bleeding feet and fed him bread and milk while we girls made him a fresh bed of straw and Daddy skinned the badger.

"This hide should bring us a few dollars," Daddy said as he showed it to us stretched out on a board. It looked even larger dead than alive.

The next morning, Fritz's eyes were swollen shut, and he had pulled the bandages from his feet. He licked his sores all day and never offered to move from his bed.

As soon as he recovered, he had the killing addiction in his blood and was ready to attack anything which ran down a hole. Often when he saw a squirrel or chuck running for its burrow, he outran and killed it, having no respect for life, premises, or ownership.

One night after dark, we heard Fritz barking and growling in the grove near our house. Daddy went to the door and called him, but he refused to come. The next morning when Daddy got up, poor Fritz had porcupine quills so thick in his flesh he looked like a pine tree. He had quills in the inside of his mouth, in his feet, and in his face. His craving to kill had dictated the wrong animal. Daddy tried to hold him down, but he couldn't get close to him.

"Berla, get up quick and help me!" Daddy said, as he banged the door open and ran for his pliers. "Fritz Yellowhair has been in a fight with a porcupine."

Daddy performed a painful, gruesome, operation, but Mama held Fritz and talked patiently all the while Daddy pulled quills. Many days passed before Fritz even so much as barked at a tree squirrel.

For several winters before Fritz came to be a steady boarder at our house, we would sit by the window at night with the light out on moonlight nights and count the jack rabbits as they came off the hill and went to the haystacks to feed. They had a hard-beaten path off the hill. Many nights as we sat with our noses pressed against the cold window, we counted as many as one hundred-fifty rabbits. They started their trek as soon as dusk fell on the mountains, and for one and a half hours, they entertained us well. This went on and on every moonlight winter night. Daddy tried many methods of killing them, but they multiplied faster than gun could shoot, poison could kill, or traps could catch.

On one particular winter night several months after the badger episode, as we watched the rabbits come down, Daddy decided to try something different. He put on his sheep-lined coat and overshoes and started toward the haystack, Fritz at his side.

The snow was crusted so hard that it crunched under foot and glistened like a myriad of stars from the reflection of the big, round, full moon.

Pulling some hay loose at the base of the stack, he situated himself and dog in the hole and watched Fritz in his excitement when the rabbits started coming.

He had a hard time teaching the dog to be quiet. "Shhh, my boy! He spoke in a whisper as he petted him and clamped his hand around his snout to keep him from barking. Fritz caught on fast and sat on his back haunches beside his master in the hole until the rabbits arrived in hordes to begin their feed, then whacking Fritz across the rump, Daddy gave him his signal to commence his kill.

Grabbing a rabbit by the back of the neck, Fritz gave it a flip, broke its back and went for another one. Rabbits panicked all over the place. They jumped, darted hither and yon, but Fritz killed eleven the first night.

The next night, they went back to the same haystack, but only a few rabbits appeared. We children watched them come off the hill and counted well over a hundred again, but when Daddy and Fritz came home about eleven o'clock with only two rabbits, Mama said, "What's the matter, Jim, did the dog let you down?"

"Nope, the rabbits out-smarted us, and all went to another haystack."

Fritz became so wise he knew the exact minute the rabbits were to trail. He would whine, paw on the kitchen door, coaxing his master to come. Daddy tried many times to send Fritz without him, but he didn't approve. He hadn't been trained that way, so Daddy and dog went hunting every night to keep the rabbit population down, except on blizzardy nights, and on that kind of nights, the rabbits didn't come down either.

Nearly every night, they had to change haystacks to keep the rabbits fooled. Sometimes the rabbits changed too, to keep Daddy and Fritz fooled.

Within a month, we could tell there were a lot fewer rabbits and within two months, Fritz had reduced the rabbit population to the extent it was no longer entertaining to count them when they came off the hill to feed, as maybe two would come; then it would be twenty minutes or half an hour before another one would be seen.

Daddy skinned and stretched each rabbit fur, shipped it to a hide and fur place far away, and received from ten to twenty-five cents for each hide. He usually waited until he would have from fifty to one hundred hides before shipping them. The company refunded the postage with the check for the furs. The money derived from these hides furnished great help for our living, and Fritz Yellowhair proved his worth.

"I believe we are gradually getting rid of the rabbits," Berla," Daddy said one day at the dinner table. "We have either got them all or they are being winter killed. They would starve to death if they didn't feed from the haystacks. This is one of the toughest winters for survival we have had yet."

"How deep is the snow now?," Mama asked. "I know it has never before been to the tops of the windows as it is now. It makes it terrifically dark in here. I can hardly see what I'm doing half the time, and today it seems even worse, as I am getting another terrible headache." She reached for a cold washrag and wiped her forehead.

"Well, it must be seven or eight feet deep in the drifts. Even the tallest fences around the stacks are completely covered," Daddy answered, as he pushed himself away from the table and asked to be excused. "Now Berla, you go lie down. The kids and I will do the dishes."

We all agreed, and led Mama to the bedroom.

"I'll wash," said Daddy, "if you kids gather up, dry and put away."

We laughed as he rolled his shirt and underwear sleeves to the elbows, for we knew when he got to the pots and pans he would have to go water the horses. It was a trick he played on us many times before we got wise enough to figure out just why horses had to be watered at a certain time on certain days.

We were making progress fast and joking when, sure enough, Daddy said, "Here, you kids take over. I've got to go water the horses."

He went to the barn, got Dan and Bally, and led them to the creek where he chopped a hole through the ice so they could drink.

Before long, he came back into the house. "Are you awake, Berla?," he whispered to Mama.

"Yes, what is it?"

"I swear a thousand head of elk are headed this way. The east hills are dotted with them. If it isn't rabbits, it's elk which gnaw on us while we are still alive."

That night, he took Meat-in-the-pot with him and climbed to the top of the nearest haystack. Just at dark, the thundering herd moved in. Daddy shot several times over their heads, but this only scattered them. They had come for food and with determination to stay. The big bulls, with their sharp horns and hooves, dug the hay from the stacks, cluttered the stackyards, permitting the whole herd to feed until spring.

Not only Daddy and Fritz, but all the neighbors and their dogs, guarded haystacks day and night, but what could they gain against thousands of "determined not to starve" elk?

Elk Herd   *K.F. Roahen, Billings, Montana*
                              U.S. Fish and Wildlife Service

Chapter XII
POLLIWOGS AND PICKLES

Seldom was a day ever planned ahead; things just happened in a natural way at "Poverty Flats." And seldom did Mama know from one hour to the next what Daddy would be doing.

We children had gone to the tool-shed to watch him sharpen his sickles for his mowing machine. There he sat, astraddle a wooden frame, treading with his feet to turn the big whetstone wheel. He held the blade close to the stone, and we loved to watch the sparks fly.

Being completely engrossed in a thing, Daddy could dismiss it so quickly and run to something else so fast, he kept us in bewilderment most of the time.

Fairly running to the house, he announced to Mama he thought he would go to Bill McInelly's to help saw wood. It was much easier for two men to saw together than one man alone. One saw was used with a handle on either end. One man stood on one side of the log and the other man on the other side. In rhythm, one pulled while the other pushed. Many pieces of firewood could be cut in this manner in a day, and besides that, sawing wood furnished an excuse for neighbors to get together once in awhile to discuss crops, irrigation, or weather, and exchange fishing and hunting stories. And never did any two men get together on Flat Creek without discussing what might be done to keep the elk herds away from their haystacks before another winter.

Daddy knew Mr. McInelly had been to town the day before and had heard the town news so he could hardly wait to talk with him.

Mama surprised Daddy by putting on a clean apron, washing children's faces, putting clean pinafore dresses on us three girls and clean shirts on Archie and Earl. We were all standing by the gate by the time Daddy got there with

Dan, Bally, and Lumber Wagon.

"Where do you think you're going?" Daddy asked in a perplexing voice.

"I'm going to take the children, and the horses, and Lumber Wagon, and we are going to visit Jane Goe and her children while you saw wood and chew words with Bill," Mama replied in a very confident manner.

"Do you think you can handle Dan and Bally all by yourself?" Daddy asked.

"As tame as these horses are, they can handle themselves," Mama replied.

Daddy lifted an eyebrow in acceptance and reached for Archie and Earl, then took Mama's hand to help her into the wagon box. We girls were also lifted up while Daddy was explaining, "If ever you would plan ahead Berla, I would be prepared for you and the children. I could have some clean hay in the wagon and you could sit in comfort. Now you'll have to sit on the bare boards, or stand up all the way, because I took the seats out yesterday."

Mama made a comeback with, "Yes, 'twould be nice to plan ahead, wouldn't it, Jim?"

We had a rough ride, and I wished all the way for that hay or a quilt to keep the shock from jarring my teeth.

When Daddy got off at McInelly's, he cautioned Mama about being careful, how to tie the horses, and all the "old stuff." We still had another mile or more to ride the bucking Lumber Wagon, but Mama handled Dan and Bally like a veteran at handling horses.

Mama warned us before we got to Goe's to stay away from the swimming hole. She was afraid of any waterhole deeper than ankle-deep. Benny, Bill and Byron had dug a large hole about fifteen feet deep and twice as wide, filled it from an irrigation ditch and learned to swim and dive like fish. Louise could swim by holding onto a board and paddling her feet. Her brothers had taught her this trick so she could save herself in water and at the same time learn to swim.

Having seen the team coming, Louise came down the dusty road a long way to meet us. Mama lifted her into the wagon, and we were so happy to meet we hugged and kissed each other all the rest of the way to their house.

Bill and Byron weren't home when we got there. We were glad for this as they, being older than we, teased us all the time. Mrs. Goe came out to help Mama tie the horses to the hitching post. She was very grateful for company.

"Land sakes, what brought you all this way along? You are certainly brave, Berla, to drive the team so far. Come on in, I've just taken some hot biscuits from the oven."

Spreading some of the hot bread with freshly churned butter, she then sprinkled the top with sugar and handed each of us girls a piece of the best smelling bread we had ever smelled. As we anxiously reached for it, Mama invited us to go outside to eat so we wouldn't spill any crumbs on the floor. We knew this was an excuse to get rid of us so they could share secrets. I never could imagine what Mama knew which could only be shared with another woman. I couldn't understand either, why we couldn't listen because even if we heard their secrets, a secret was a secret so long as it was never repeated and therefore had to remain as such with us as we never saw anyone to share it with. Nevertheless, we went out to play.

After our hot biscuits were eaten, we caught polliwogs. Mr. Goe and the boys had been digging post holes, and in every one we found from two to six. They would hop in, but couldn't hop out. We put them in an old rusty, enameled teakettle with a wide spout and a lid. When we got the kettle about half full, we tried pouring them out to see how many could make it through the spout and how many got stuck. By the time we shook the teakettle hard many times to get the next polliwog through, we had polliwog soup inside.

We had a singular purpose that day—fun! So our next episode took place in Mrs. Goe's cellar where she had a crockery jar of dill pickles brewing. We decided to have a contest to see which one could eat the most pickles. Rinsing the polliwogs off our hands in the ditch, we plunged into the jar, four hands at once.

At first, the dill pickles looked like polliwogs crammed in that jar and I wasn't so sure they didn't taste like polliwogs. After the third pickle apiece, we decided that game had to end. Louise suggested we visit the granary where her parents had some elk jerky hanging. We took one long string of it down from the hook and took turns chewing on either end.

Mrs. Goe came to the door and called us to come in and have some lunch. We all declined, saying we weren't hungry.

Mama then came to call. "Come on girls, Mrs. Goe has the nicest lunch. She has dill pickles and jerky, you know how you like these."

"We don't want to eat," we all kept shouting, until finally they decided to let us play.

Feeling as if we had all the lunch we needed for one day, Louise suggested we have a swim. I protested saying Mama had strictly told us we were to stay away from the swimming hole. Margaret said she, too, must obey, but Louise kept saying the hole had only a little bit of water in it and we could go wading. We went to the pool to investigate and found it true. Louise said she would go in first and show us it was only up to her waist. She stripped off all her clothes and grabbed her little board and paddled off. Erma decided it looked fun, so she stripped, too, so Mama wouldn't see her wet clothes.

Margaret and I begged Erma to stay on the bank, but she waded in. Erma, the brave, bold one of us, seemed always willing to do anything anyone suggested, so long as it sounded like fun or adventure. She waded right out to the middle of the pool. She was shorter than Louise so the water struck her just at her armpits. She jumped around in the water with her arms outstretched to balance herself, and she looked just like a little fairy with her long hair floating on top as she giggled with every jump.

Louise offered Erma her board, but Erma said, "I'm having more fun just like this." Then, calling to the bank, "I have two sissy sisters. Come on, Margaret and Bertha, you can see how safe this is, and Mama will never know if you take your clothes off."

Bill and Byron came in from the field and decided to take a swim to refresh themselves, then remembered they had drained the pool the day before; so they opened the headgate which let a gush of water in the pool all at once, forming a vortex. We could see the sudden flow of water pouring in, but didn't have the slightest knowledge of where it was coming from, nor how to stop it. Erma panicked and tried to reach Louise with the board. Louise paddled to Erma, but her board wouldn't hold both of them, because in her fright Erma tried to climb right on top of it. By now, they both panicked because the water was up to their shoulders and still rushing in. Margaret and I stood on the bank screaming. We knew we had to do something, but what? We didn't have time to get Mama and Mrs. Goe and no one else was in sight. Erma grabbed Louise around the neck and both girls went under.

By this time, Bill and Byron had reached the pool. Screaming and crying hysterically, all we could do was to point to the water and yell, "Get 'em Bill, get 'em Bill!" Bill pulled off his shoes and plunged into the water, clothes and all, and dived to the bottom of the pool. When he came up, he had a girl in each arm. They were spitting and choking, but we could tell they were still alive and breathing. Upon discovering they were nude, Bill dropped them at the edge

104

of the bank, snickered, and ran.

Mama knew readily that one of her daughters had disobeyed her. Erma, while running her hands through her long, wet hair and trembling with fright, revealed all. Mama said very little. She knew Erma had learned a lesson.

That night, after we were safely home, had supper, and had done the dishes, Mama asked Daddy what he and Bill had discussed.

"Mostly elk problems all day," he replied.

"Come, girls, I'll help you get into bed. You have had a busy day," Mama said as she put her arms around us and led us to our bedroom upstairs. She listened to our prayers while we thanked the Lord we still had a little sister and friend Louise.

I didn't sleep well that night, as I had cramps in my tummy and hurt all over from mixed emotions and excitement. After all, a day away from home was excitement enough to keep me awake, let alone polliwogs, dill pickles and jerky; and I realized Erma felt even worse than I, as she had swimming pool water mixed with hers.

Chapter XIII
AUNT WOODA

It seems that trials, worries, surprises, tribulations and explorations never ceased at our place.

Mama had written her sister Ruby, a nurse, inviting her to come stay a month with us. Daddy brought in Slumber Tuff, our folding bed, from the tool shed where it had been stored, and put it up in the kitchen for us three girls. Aunt Ruby was to occupy our bed.

Truly an exciting experience we had the day we went to town to meet Aunt Ruby. We got up in time to greet the dawn. I had never heard the birds sing so sweetly, so early, because I had never been up that early before, except the day we went over Teton Pass in winter. I discovered I had been missing something in beauty and color. Mama told us we had been sleeping the most beautiful part of the day away, that birds always sing the sweetest just before sun-up, and in order to capture the full flavor of this experience, it was necessary to get up before daybreak.

Daddy milked Curley, early, while Mama cooked a delicious breakfast for us, but I couldn't eat a bite. I was too excited. Today we got to go to town—and today we had company coming—one of our favorite aunts.

Erma was gifted with a special way of wagging, and twisting her tongue, and putting forth words in a language all her own. When she was a tiny, little girl, she couldn't pronounce Ruby, so she twisted it to Wooda—so today we were to meet Aunt Wooda.

Far behind us to the east, we could see the sun rising over Whistler's Peak as Daddy, Margaret, Erma, and I left home in Lumber Wagon. Daddy had bobbed the tails of Dan and Bally. They too felt frisky so early in the morning. We sang all the songs we knew, counted all the gophers and rockchucks we saw and wished we had a penny or a nickel for each one.

Arriving in town two hours later, in time to meet the stage from Idaho, we stood on the board steps of the hotel waiting, so impatiently and excitedly that we were trembling.

The closed-in carriage finally arrived, drawn by four beautiful, jet-black, cantering horses, with their tails braided and bobbed. Their harnesses glistened with silver mountings.

As the horses approached the hitching post, their strength, speed, and spirit was breathtaking. Mr. Scott gave a sharp command—"Whoa!" Every horse brought all four feet to a halt in perfect unison. I was moved by his perfection in handling the horses. Even though he had been driving about five hours and was weary, he politely opened the door of the stagecoach, after he had stretched, shook his legs, yawned, and swung his arms to release the circulation to his tired hands.

I knew this was the same teamster who had driven us over Teton Pass. I could tell by the scars, and the smile on his face. Displaying both tradition and style, he wore a black cap, a swallow tailed coat with brass buttons, black britches and shiny black boots.

We all stepped close to the stagecoach so we could look in, and out stepped a huge, burly, unshaven man, smoking a big cigar. We began to wonder if Aunt Wooda could survive such a trip as that one, over the mountainous road, cooped up in a coach with a big cigar, and a worldly character who would stand six feet in his socks. We were almost relieved to discover she wasn't on the stage, but what to do now? The driver knew nothing of her.

Daddy suggested we go to the telephone and telegraph office to see if any message had come through. There we found out that the line was out of order over the mountain and no message could be sent. Mr. Lovejoy, a jolly, little thin man, slight of stature, with an effeminate voice, and gray hair, definitely showing his many years, was the sole owner and operator of the telephone and telegraph company of the town and all outlying districts. He assured Daddy that he had a man out trying to find the trouble.

Taking Erma by one hand, me by the other, and Margaret trotting along by my side, Daddy took us to the store to buy us a piece of candy. Store candy was something we had seldom tasted.

Greeting Mr. DeLoney as we entered the store, Daddy said, "Hi Pap! Just came to buy the kids a piece of candy."

As Pap arose from his chair where he had been reading his newspaper, he glanced over the rims of his spectacles and said, "Now, Jim, you didn't just come to town to get the kids a piece of candy. What is so urgent today?"

Being so amazed at all I could see, I forgot to notice what kind of candy my sisters were choosing. I gawked around with my mouth wide open, looking at horse collars, gas lanterns, rope, tin tubs, and boilers hanging from the top of the walls; crockery jars with pickles, barrels of crackers, boxes of dried apricots, apples and prunes, and lots of canned foods were stacked on the shelves. On a big long table were heaps of overalls and coveralls. You could tell the girls wear from the boys because each pair of girls had a pin or button on the pocket and a drop seat behind. Bars of Naptha soap were stacked high with a piece of parchment paper between bars. Homemade butter laid on the counter and the lady's name who made it accompanied each pound. My eyes then traveled to a tool and gun rack and next to this were bolts of cloth and sewing notions. I was trying to smell the bottles of perfume when Daddy said, "Come girls, let's get out of here and go see the rest of the town."

Town consisted of one brick adobe store where we bought the candy; one blacksmith shop where a large, brawny man stood constantly bent over the hoof of a horse, fitting a shoe to its foot; a post office and butcher shop

108

combined, where a happy-go-lucky man came to wait on his customers, chewing the butt-end of a cigar and wiping his fingers on a blood-stained, white butcher apron; a drugstore where a quiet, sober gentleman worked away, filling prescriptions or churning ice cream. A dance hall stood above the drugstore, where on Saturday nights many a fiddler fiddled away, and many a young man danced with his pretty colleen. Near the store stood a shoe cobbler's shop. The cobbler fixed everything from shoes to harnesses; so long as it was made of leather, and he could use either thread or rivets, the article was mended like new. And off to itself stood a livery stable. Often on cold nights, horses were taken there while the owner danced or visited. A small printing office, where the local newspaper was printed once a month, stood off to itself too.

Children from six to twenty attended school in one building. It had eight rooms; four on the ground floor and four upstairs. A big white pelican hung from the ceiling in one room upstairs. It had been shot by a hunter, stuffed, and donated to the school. When a pupil got enough promotions to be permitted to go where the pelican hung, he felt very well-educated.

Through a lot of persuasion on the part of kind Doctor Huff, labor and donations from citizens, a tiny little hospital was erected. A few board sidewalks, with wide cracks between each board, joined the path from one business place to another. There were three humble churchhouses, which stood lonely and forlorn, but were visited and occupied each Sunday by the Christians of the village. There were also two small hotels, one of brick, and one of frame. The little telephone office completed the town and gave it that "modern touch."

After taking most of these places in, we spent the rest of the day sitting on a hard-slabbed, wooden bench, awaiting some word.

While there, we observed every move the telephone operator made. When the switchboard gave a buzzing sound, he would push a plug in a little hole, and a light would come on and he would say, "Central."

No one had a telephone number. The person placing the call would answer by saying, "Will you please buzz Mr. so-and-so?"

Mr. Lovejoy would answer back, "I'll try, but I think he went fishing today." Or he would say, "He isn't home. I just saw him ride through town on a horse." He knew all the news and if anyone wanted to find out anything from the time of day to when his neighbor was going to be home, he would call Mr. Lovejoy to find out.

Or, if anyone left home for any length of time, he would call the operator and say, "I'm going to be gone a few days so if anybody tries to get in touch with me, tell him I'm away. I'll call you when I get home."

At one p.m., we ate the lunch Mama had packed. Daddy mentioned we had better go to the wagon to eat, but Mr. Lovejoy insisted Daddy get the lunch and let us eat inside where it was comfortable.

After lunch, Erma curled up on the bench and went to sleep, then Margaret and I didn't have a place to sit, so we went outside and sat on the steps and watched the passers-by.

At nine o'clock that evening, the big light above the switchboard came on. Mr. Lovejoy said, "The trouble has been found and the line over the mountain is back in working order."

Daddy placed a long distance call to another Aunt in Idaho, and Aunt Wooda answered the call. She had been trying to send a message all day to let us know my cousin, LeRoy Kearsley, the one who had teased me about my Tom-Thumbs, had been killed by lightening, and that was the reason she didn't come on the stage that morning. She said she intended to stay there with Aunt Lula and help out all she could until after the funeral. I heard Daddy say, I hate to go home and tell Berla. She will go all to pieces, but I'll do my best with her, and do hurry, Ruby! She needs you."

The long, long journey home that night wasn't half so pleasant returning as it had been going.

Still up, of course and burning Carrie, Mama sat listening for Daddy's whistle.

Erma said she never wanted to go on another vacation.

After getting a letter in the mail from Aunt Wooda, Daddy went to town four days later, once more to meet the stage, but this time he went alone—and this time she was there. They were back home by noon and found Mama sick. We thought she was still upset over the death of her nephew.

Mama told Aunt Wooda that Grandma McInelley's son, Jim, and his wife, Opal, were staying at McInelly's and living in a tent, helping Bill with the haying, and Opal surely wanted to see her.

The next morning Mama felt quite well, so Aunt Wooda took a short cut and walked through stubble where the hay had just been taken from the field. We girls begged to go with her, but she said she had better go alone this time, but would take us another time if she went. We watched her until she disappeared around a haystack which obscured our view of the McInelly house. She stayed all day, which perturbed me. I thought she had come to visit us and not the McInellys.

That night, Jim McInnelly brought her home on his horse, she riding sidesaddle, and Jim walking. It was after dark and Mama had been coaxing us to go to bed, but we couldn't go until Aunt Wooda got home.

She came in so excited, clapping her hands together. "Guess what?" she said. I hated that game by now, because I never could guess right, but we guessed she got lost and couldn't find her way back home. We guessed she had been kidnapped and about every other exciting thing we could think of .

"No, now just listen carefully and I'll tell you a big story. While I was on my way to see Opal McInelly this morning, I stopped right down there by that haystack," she said, using her pointer finger to emphasize the exact haystack, "to clean the stubble out of my shoes and I heard the queerest noise. I listened and I thought I could hear a little animal of some kind. Then I heard it again and I went around the stack to the south end and there was a tiny, little brand new baby girl."

"Oh, Aunt Wooda, what did you do with it?," we all asked in unison. Erma's eyes looked as if they were going to pop right out of their sockets.

"Well, I gathered the sweet little thing up in my apron and took her on with me and when I got to McInelly's, Opal wanted the baby so bad, I gave it to her. She is going to name her Louise."

"Oh!—Aunt Wooda! Why didn't you keep her?," I asked so sorrowfully. "We have all those baby clothes ready for the poor Belgians."

"You see dear, I'm not married," she said, "and it isn't right for a woman to have a baby unless she is married.

"Well, you could give it to Mama, she's married," said Margaret.

"I don't think your Mama wants another girl, do you Berla?," asked Aunt Ruby.

"No, because when we get another baby, we want a boy don't we?" Mama asked waiting for the affirmative answer.

Aunt Ruby walked back to McInelly's the next morning to bathe the new baby and the mama. We couldn't figure out why the mama couldn't bathe herself and her new baby too. We warned Aunt Ruby if she found another baby in the haystack it was to be ours, boy or girl, and for her not to dare take another baby anywhere.

Funny thing though, she never did find another one. She

said that night when she returned home that she had searched every haystack along the way, both going and coming, but she couldn't find a baby. One of these days, she thought she might find one somewhere.

In town lived a little Jewish man who heard about Aunt Ruby being a nurse and staying with us. His name was Sam and he wanted to get married so bad he had proposed to about every eligible girl around. Hearing about this new single girl, he rode up on horseback one day to visit us. It was very obvious why he had come. He didn't take his eyes off Aunt Ruby, which made her very nervous.

"What did that old goat really come for?," she asked as soon as he had gone.

"Well, if it's what I think," said Mama, "you'll be seeing a lot more of him."

She did. He made trip after trip and each time brought pretty jewels, candy or flowers with him. He became an epidemic.

One day, about ten o'clock, Aunt Ruby saw him coming and just had time to dive under the bed, where she was forced to remain the rest of the day. Sam, being as persistent as she, stayed until dark.

Erma started calling him Uncle Sam, thinking he was our uncle. This made Aunt Ruby furious so we changed his name and called him Aunt Sam.

Several nights after Aunt Wooda "found" Opal's baby, we had an exciting time at our house. Erma and I had been outside playing and she threw a rock, which hit me in the forehead. The next I knew I was lying on Feather Tuff, and Aunt Wooda was putting cold packs on my head.

I finally asked Aunt Wooda where Mama was, and she said, "In the bedroom, sick dear."

I got up to see her. She assured me she felt fine, so I went back to bed and because of all the excitement I had terrible nightmares. I dreamed I had a stick and I hit the ground, and as I did, I counted one—and then the earth trembled and a sound of "boom" rolled forth. I counted two—another tremble and another sound of "boom" rolled forth. I counted this way to ten and just as I said "ten," the whole earth opened up with the most terrible "BOOM" I have ever heard.

The next morning when I awakened, I had two surprises—one was I found out in my dream, just as I said, "ten," and the earth exploded, Daddy had shot a big pack-rat right over our heads on the headboard on Feather Tuff. The rat had been giving us a bad time for a week. Daddy saw his opportunity to get him, so he did. The other surprise was—I had a new baby brother.

Chapter XIV
HOLIDAYS ON FLAT CREEK

Any Sunday we could coax Daddy into taking us to church in town, we considered a holiday. Mama had the most unique way of working Daddy without his knowing it.

One Friday, Mama baked a gooseberry pie, Daddy's favorite dish. After he had eaten his first piece and asked for the second helping, Mama cut another piece and as she dished it up on his plate said, "Jim, I am so lonely, I feel like a piece of furniture glued to this floor, surrounded by four walls."

Daddy replied, "Well, there's no sense in getting yourself all lonely now. I have to sharpen posts all day today. Might as well get the fences ready to put up around haystacks as soon as the hay is up. I want to be prepared to keep the pesky elk out of the stacks as long as I can this coming winter."

Mama said, "I'm not thinking about today, but Sunday I surely would love to go to church."

"Church?" Daddy yelled. "You know church is a luxury around here."

"I know," said Mama, "but so long as it doesn't cost anything to go. I think we should be there once in a while."

Getting up from the table, Daddy excused himself, put on his hat and went to sharpen fence posts.

The next day, Mama asked Daddy to kill a couple of chickens. She said she wanted them for Sunday dinner. She boiled them, cut all the meat off the bones, moistened the meat with the soup and set it to jell. Then she made a big gingerbread cake. That night, each of us children was tubbed and scrubbed and Mama put her hair and ours up in rags. She confidentially told us she had a feeling Daddy would be taking us to Sunday School.

Sunday morning, Mama got up early to make sand-

115

wiches from the chicken. We girls were dressed in our pretty plaid dresses with matching ribbons in our hair. The boys had on little pongee shirts, boe-ties, and knee pants.

When Daddy came in from doing the chores, he looked us over and asked in a puzzling voice, just as if he couldn't guess, "What is going on here? Where do you all think you are going?"

Mama tried to explain to him that she had told him two days ago we were all going to church next Sunday, "And this is next Sunday."

When Daddy saw the sandwiches being wrapped and the cake put in a clean flour sack, he realized the only way he could have any of it was to go along.

After Sunday School, the ladies spread a big table with a white cloth, put the lunch out together and each mother dished her children's plates and set them on benches. "Just like a picnic to us," we thought.

Following lunch, we all went back for another session of church. This lasted for two hours. Daddy said on his way home, "I'm sure glad I went. Old man Curtis gave the best talk I have ever heard."

Mama knew it would be another month or so before she could figure out another shenanigan that might work to get us to church again.

When the first Sunday in July rolled around, Daddy curried his horses, combed their manes, and braided and bobbed their tails. Two seats were put in Lumber Wagon instead of one and a bed of hay in the bottom of the box for the boys to sit on, and we headed for the Flat Creek picnic grounds, for this was an event not to be missed.

Every year on the first Sunday in July, all the Flat Creek folks would gather at the picnic grounds with baskets of fried chicken, hot biscuits, potato salads, homemade crockery dill pickles, punch, gingerbread cake and churned ice cream. The carryings on there for a rounded six hours

116

consisted of contests of horseshoe-throwing, and a final game of baseball between fathers and sons. About the only contest the women folk could enter was to see who could have the most children present each year. The Haights, Kellys, Moodys, Ben Goes, George Goes, Van Leerdams, Petersens, Seatons, Curtis, Hanshews, Wrights, and Chambers could produce a fine crop of young ones, and each year, about six new babies would be present. Grandma McInelly and her son, Bill, were always present. Grandma, as everyone called her, was a sweet, gregarious, charming soul, so old her wrinkles were as deep as Nakoni Teoni's, but she had as much fun as anyone. She originally came from England. Talking with an accent, her favorite phrase was, "Ah, now wouldn't that make a preacher want to cuss?" Mr. and Mrs. Webster LaPlante came from quite a distance, but they were nearly always first to arrive. They had no children, but loved to watch the antics of others. The widow Simpson, with her three children, Chester, Arthur, and Lizzy were nearly always second.

Everyone lined up after the picnics, out in the open, away from the trees to where the sun shone brightly, for a picture. Families were usually grouped together so when the younger ones grew up, they could be identified.

One day at the picnic, Mama was the recipient of the prize. She had the most children, and by adding one every two years, she took the prize each year thereafter. Mr. Moody passed the hat and Mama received four dollars. Someone remarked this was the pay-off for such a fine crop of young 'uns, but Mama let him know right away her pay-off couldn't be counted in money, but in blessings she received from the joy of her family.

It seemed that the boys far outnumbered the girls at the picnics, but the girls made a good showing for themselves. Each year, every girl went to the picnic with a new hat. Each mother tried to dress her daughters as pretty as possible, then all day they admonished the girls to be careful not to soil their pretty dresses. We were reminded several times during the day that we were girls and should act like young ladies.

Frankie Petersen, with the longest legs, always won the foot race. His sister, Martha, took the prize each year for being able to sit on a post the longest without help.

Tree limbs made convenient supporting places to put baby jumpers while mothers stood close by preparing the picnic, at the same time trying to protect their little ones from mosquitoes and deerflies.

There being no tables available, quilts were spread out on the ground, then pretty tablecloths spread on top, the food put all together in the center and served in one big family style. The party usually began about ten o'clock a.m. or as soon as any two families got there. It lasted until four p.m. as everyone had a long way to go home and chores were waiting.

Perhaps a little secret envy would have been felt by others had they known the fun they missed by not belonging to the Flat Creek territory.

A promise made by either Daddy or Mama gave us the assurance it would be carried out to its exact fullness if we children kept our part of the bargain. Daddy wanted to try riding Old Doll—a white mare given to him by Uncle Thomas Perry—to town to try her out. Uncle Thomas said he couldn't keep her any longer as she threw his boys so many times he was afraid of killing one of them sometime. So Daddy saddled her and off they went. This was in June and he had some urgent business to attend to while there, but before going, promised if we would help Mama cheerfully that day he would bring us a surprise from town.

One of the prominent businessmen invited him to visit the fairgrounds. He did so and stayed six hours to help erect a grandstand. By the means of big scoops, horsedrawn, and manhandled, the ground had been cleared of sagebrush; a project well-commenced for a lot of future recreations.

By the Fourth of July, the fairgrounds were completed, broncs were rounded up, cowboys had volunteered to ride any beast which could be caught.

When Daddy got home that night, he didn't have a treat for us. We couldn't figure out what the promise made could be.

"How did you and Doll get along?" was Mama's first inquiry.

"Splendid," Daddy said, "but she shies at every little tin can, bottle or even a noise."

"What is our surprise?" we all wanted to know.

"Well sir, there's a frontier coming to town so I saved the money for treats and decided to take all of you on the Fourth of July."

When Mama heard this, she went to Rainy Day and counted her excess change, knowing no other money was available, then exclaimed, "Why Jim! How can you make such a promise to our children? We don't even have the price of admittance."

Smiling, Daddy raised his eyebrows. He knew he had Mama guessing.

"Jim, you know they will be disappointed. I don't even have any eggs to sell because six of our ten hens are setting."

After a long silence, broken only by the grin on Daddy's face, Mama said, "Sir Hon! You had better have an ace up your sleeve or apologize now."

Daddy finally said, "I have worked out our admittance by helping build the grandstand. Everyone working on it or the grounds get in free with his family this first time."

"But how will this affect our annual Flat Creek picnic?" Mama asked, turning the calendar over to take a look at July.

"Not at all Berla. I already looked ahead and the Fourth of July comes on Thursday this year so that will give us three days in between the frontier and the picnic."

All this while we children stood motionless awaiting the verdict.

The morning of the Fourth, not a cloud could be seen and through the eyes of a child all the world looked beautiful.

We each were dressed in our best outfit, the same we wore to Church and the same we would be wearing three days later, so we were warned over and over again to act like ladies.

Rigged up high on a tall pole, we saw a big horn and we could hear the voice of a man coming loud and clear through it.

"The parade is about to commence," the voice said. "All entries are lining up at the gate. Step right up to the ticket booth and purchase your tickets now to avoid the rush."

Reaching to his inside vest pocket, Daddy pulled a slip of paper out and said, "Here Berla, take this and the kids over to the ticket booth, then get a good seat," and pointing about halfway up in the grandstand, "about there where we can get the best view of the track, and I'll tie the horses in the shade and join you soon."

The steps were so far apart for our little legs, we were compelled to crawl up them on all fours.

"Be careful of the slivers," Mama said, "and watch your pretty dresses."

By now, the grandstand was filling with people who seemed to know one another. Curried, combed and decorated horses pranced around the brown, oval arena, pulling beautiful rigs—white tops with fringe all around on some, balloons flying from others, ribbons and bows made beautiful the wheels.

A covered wagon entered the arena, drawn by one large horse and one very small one, just as the parade went out the east gate. It was the "treat" wagon, full of ice cream

120

freezers, lemonade, popcorn balls, and Lillian DeLoney's professionally made candy. My mouth watered as the announcer told what the wagon contained. Lillian DeLoney made the best candy in all the world, the people of Jackson thought.

Opening a little black bag, Mama gave us each a dime and told us we could spend that much, but warned us to spend a nickel of it at a time, because we might get thirsty when the day became hotter in the afternoon. Taking little brothers by the hand, we visited the "treat" wagon.

Several cowboys tried their luck on broncs, steers, and bulldogging calves, but finally a challenge came.

"Anyone here willing to try his luck on Indian Killer?," the announcer asked.

Everyone began to stand up to see if anyone would accept the challenge. Every cowboy present stepped forward to take a look at Indian Killer in his stall, but everyone jumped off the gate, shaking his head. Indian Killer looked vicious and mean.

"We offer ten dollars to anyone who will try and fifteen to anyone who rides him until the whistle blows."

Stepping out in the ring, with his hat in his hand, a handsome cowboy with chaps and spurs shouted, "I'll ride him or die." It was Walt Spicer who spoke these brave words.

The audience shouted and clapped. Some whistled, then the clown entered the ring, riding backwards on a donkey. He pulled many funny tricks while the bronc handlers were getting Indian Killer tamed down enough for Walt to straddle him.

Another young lad, one who considered himself a man, at the age of seventeen, seemed to be interested in everything that went on. He helped get Indian Killer ready. His father, seeing the danger, ran to the chutes and yelled, "Bob, Bob Crisp, you come here right now! You may get hurt."

Bob, standing on the top rail of the chute, waved his cowboy hat at his father and replied, "Dad, I'm supposed to be here, I am one of the participants." Thus started his long career of being a professional cowboy.

The chute opened, the bronc came out biting the dirt and snorting. Walt waving his hat in the air, spurred him with every jump. He rode him to the whistle.

Each Thanksgiving, we enjoyed the company of the Goes, Grandma McInelly, Bill and the school teacher. They were our closest neighbors.

By Thanksgiving, the snow was real deep and often Daddy, Bill and Mr. Goe spent most of the day before breaking road and packing it, so the company could come to our house or we could get to the Goe's place. Grandma McInelly was Mrs. Goe's mother, so whenever it came Grandma's turn to have Thanksgiving dinner, either Mrs. Goe or Mama cooked it instead.

How we looked forward to that day in the year. The creeks were all frozen over, which made for good sledding or skating. Lyle, Louise, Bill, Byron, Margaret, Erma, and I played in the snow so long we usually had to come in and dry out by Pot-Belly stove before the Goes could go home. Florence and Benny usually preferred staying in the house to help cook the dinner or listen to our parents and the teacher visit. The teacher lived in the schoolhouse only a quarter of a mile from McInelly's so she would walk or web to their place and ride with them.

One Thanksgiving Day, when the company gathered at our house, a very amusing thing happened. Getting ready to sit up to the table, the teacher decided to help Grandma up and noticed a button undone on Grandma's blouse. She proceeded to button it, but it made Grandma angry. "Ah, lave me alone!" she commanded, in her broken English tongue.

"But you have a button undone," said the teacher.

"Ah done care if Ah 'ave," Grandma replied, at the same time getting up and taking her chair with her.

"You don't want to go to the table that way," the teacher said.

"Ah yes Ah do, Ah come this way an' Ah'll go 'ome this way," Grandma insisted.

All the rest of the day the teacher tried to sneak behind Grandma to button the blouse, but Grandma kept her eyes wide open and as she promised, she did go home that way.

Another Thanksgiving Day just the Goe family came to our house and that day ended sorrowfully. The Goes were on their way home. Mama stood at the window watching them, wondering if it would be spring before she would have a good visit with Mrs. Goe again. Something spooked the horses and they began to run. They left the packed road and ran in circles through the deep snow. Within seconds, the sleigh box flew off the bobs with the whole family in it. Mr. Goe threw the lines when he could see he couldn't hold the horses. The bobs uncoupled, leaving the back bob in the field, lightening the load so the horses could run all the faster. They ran until there wasn't a thing left of their outfit but the harnesses, singletrees, and part of the tongue.

"Come quick, Jim!" Mama shouted to Daddy as she saw the horses break into the run. "They may all be killed. Do something Jim, do something!"

Daddy ran for his team and sleigh. The horses were in the corral and it didn't take him long to throw their harnesses on. When he reached the scene of the accident, Mr. and Mrs. Goe were standing with their children all huddled together trying to see if there were any broken bones. Louise had a nose bleed and a bump on her forehead. Lyle, holding her side, said it hurt. The rest seemed to be too frightened to complain. Mr. Goe, being noted all around Flat Creek as being a great horseman, now had his vanity hurt.

123

Daddy got them all in his sleigh and invited them to go back to our house, but Mrs. Goe wanted to go home. Daddy helped them into the house, tied his team to the hitching post and helped Mr. Goe and Benny catch the horses. with the means of their transportation gone, there was no question as to whether the Goes would do any more celebrating the rest of that winter or not.

Christmas was the next thing to look forward to on the ranch. Even though our gifts were very meager, we knew no differently so we were happy, no matter what our small lot.

The excitement of going with Daddy for the tree was great fun. We would start coaxing soon after Thanksgiving to go get the tree, but Mama stalled us off as long as possible, because there wasn't room for a tree in our small home, until absolutely necessary. Nevertheless, our coaxing paid off and we always got a tree a few days before Christmas. We coaxed for the biggest one in the forest, but Daddy got one to fit his taste and our house, saying, "Oh, let's let that one grow a while longer; it isn't large enough yet. These two look as if they were destined for destruction." He always got one for the school at the same time.

The real excitement came when we popped and strung popcorn for decorations.

When the tree began to look tantalizing and all white with corn, like snowballs on each branch, we danced with glee and taught baby brothers they weren't supposed to eat tree trimmings. The next few nights were spent making ornaments from colored paper given us by the teacher. Hanging each one with care up high enough so the little ones couldn't reach them, made us so proud of our artistic ability.

The mail order catalog again played an important part in our lives. Each of us studied it until it was nearly worn out before Christmas arrived. Mama carefully chose one present apiece, and promised us Santa wouldn't forget.

One Christmas, we girls each got a little golden colored

mechanical pencil with a black ribbon tied to it so we could wear it around our necks. The boys got one top and three little whistles. Another Christmas, Santa didn't forget us, but left a note in a pan of nuts saying he was sorry he ran out of presents before he reached our house, and all he had left were the nuts and one little tin horn, but this didn't stop it from being one of our special, favorite Christmases. We took turns blowing the horn, and marching around the table like little tin soldiers. We had love in our home and that gave us the spirit of Christmas.

Chapter XV
A CURE ALL FOR ALL

"I felt this thing coming on me for a week or more," Daddy said as he tried to get out of bed one morning. He had been sick all night, swollen, and in terrific pain. He fell back on the bed, shaking and shuddering.

We suspected something was wrong for several days, because whenever he sat in his favorite, high-backed, leather-padded rocker and rocked rapidly to-and-fro for many hours at a time, refusing to let us climb in with him for a free ride, we knew he was either in despair of mind or ill health.

Getting out the family doctor book, "A Cure All For All," she called it, Mama thumbed through the pages until she came to a picture of a man with swollen, inflamed joints. "Rheumatism," she said, going on to read. "Symptoms: Red, swollen joints and muscles, sore and painful. Cause: Poison in system. Treatment: Hot, wet packs to affected area. Bed rest. If not immediately relieved, see a doctor."

"Let's get started with the hot packs," Daddy said. "I can't afford to lie around here like this."

Those hot packs went on day and night for three weeks. This being in the dead of winter made it so hard for Mama to do the chores alone. She looked so funny in Daddy's bib overalls and heavy sheeplined coat as she tried to pull enough frozen hay from the stack to feed Curley, Dan, Bally, and Doll. Her hands would be nearly frozen each night and morning when she finished the chores. Each time she came in, so blue with cold, Daddy avowed he would be better by another day and do the chores himself.

"Now Jim, this isn't going to hurt me," Mama kept assuring him. "Please forget the chores and don't worry about me. Everything is well except you, so rest, and get better, that's all I ask." Then she kissed him on his forehead, stepped out of chore clothes, washed her hands, and prepared more hot packs.

Mama told us to stop at McInelly's on our way to school and ask Bill if he would go to town and get Dr. Huff. We were afraid Daddy was going to die, as he was definitely worse this morning.

I had never felt the cold more than this morning when Margaret and I went to school. Mama carefully wrapped our faces with scarfs, our legs with leggings, pulled our hoods down over our foreheads, put mittens and overshoes on, and gave us each a bottle of hot water to carry under our coats. She said, "Now girls, keep your hands on the hot bottles of water to keep your hands from freezing, and—keep moving!"

Erma stayed home, Mama fearing she couldn't make it in the cold.

By the time we got to McInelly's, both Margaret and I were crying. I felt a lump under my chin which wiggled when I moved the flesh with my hands. Grandma McInelly took us in by the stove and opened the oven door to warm us. She felt the lump and said, "Ahh, my child, you 'ave a chillblane."

Early in the afternoon, Dr. Huff stopped his little black team in front of our house. As he jumped from his one bobbed, sleigh box, he carried a robe and his black bag with him. "I am chilled to the bone. If you don't mind, I'll stand here by the stove a minute to warm my hands before I touch Jim," the doctor said. "I brought my webs along just in case—I thought I might run into some drifts here in the country."

"Please do get warm Doctor," said Mama, as she helped him out of his big fur coat. "Put your bag on this chair and I'll warm your robe and coat on the oven."

Examining Daddy, the Doctor found him all broken out with a rash, as well as swollen joints. "Rheumatism and

127

shingles both, Jim. You are going to have to have your teeth pulled. The poison is coming from them."

"Why, I never had a toothache in my life Doc!" Daddy said. "You must be mistaken."

"No, I'm not Jim. They are all loose in the gums and I tell you they are infected. I don't know who we can get to pull them though. Too bad we don't have a dentist in town."

Daddy's brother heard how sick Daddy was so he came to our rescue, bringing his fourteen-year-old sister-in-law with him. They were each riding a horse, and uncle leading one.

"I thought you might need some help, Uncle Jess said, "so I brought Hazel with me. She's a cracker-jack at handling horses and says she will enroll in school here 'till spring and can take the kids to school with her."

Mama so thankful for help, could hardly believe it when Hazel Hedrick said she would stay. Mama worried about us riding horses though, as we had ridden few in our lives.

Nancy had been trained to race. Hazel had won several prizes with her. I rode behind Hazel, on Nancy, while Margaret and Erma rode Clipper, a big, fat, tame, white mare. Hazel tried to hold Nancy back to string along with Clipper and the girls, but Nancy had high-spirited blood in her, and could see no reason in poking along with a plug mare who had little spirits, if any. If Nancy couldn't come in first, she wouldn't be in the race. This was the way Hazel had trained her, so we usually beat the other girls to school fully ten minutes. The same thing applied in going home.

Being extra-anxious one night to beat Clipper, Nancy didn't stop for the bars to be let down when we came to the fence, but to our amazement, leaped over it. Hazel stayed in the saddle, but I gathered myself up off the ground, and holding my elbow, started to cry. Just at that time, Clipper and the girls got there.

"Are you hurt?," asked Margaret.

"No, I just have a broken arm, I think."

"Well, don't just stand there and bawl, let the bars down," she said.

Nancy kept running until she got about halfway home, and Hazel managed to turn her around, calm her down enough that I could crawl on again.

"Do be careful girls," Mama warned us each morning after that, "and try to keep a firm hold on Nancy, Hazel."

Dr. Huff made another trip, three days later, to see Daddy. This time he had some strange looking tools in his little black bag. When he started to unroll them, Daddy asked, "What are you going to do with those tools Doc? You surely have intentions of using them or why else would you be unrolling them?"

The Doctor looked at Daddy and said, "I told you your teeth had to come out. I'm prepared and I hope you are."

Dr. Huff had never pulled teeth before in his life, other than maybe one at a time for some poor soul with a toothache, but all twenty-eight of Daddy's came out that day with just a little chloroform, persistence and suffering.

"Now I want you to promise me, Jim, you'll stay in bed for at least ten days. It will take that long for the poison to get out of your body. I don't like the looks of this swollen knee." Then, turning to Mama, he said, "Keep hot packs on this knee Mrs. Chambers, and always be sure it is elevated."

Mama stepped to the door to hold it open for the Doctor and to thank him again for coming and as she did she saw another herd of elk coming out of the east mountains, headed for the haystacks. She gasped, but didn't say a word. That night when she and Hazel went out to do the chores, the fields were thick with elk. They tried figuring out some possible way to scare them away form the stacks, but the snow was so deep in the fields it was impossible for them to even go where the elk were. They didn't mention a word about them to Daddy. He had enough without any added worries.

After the elk had knocked down most of the fences around the stacks, and got their bellies full, they left for the mountains just at sun-up. Mama watched them leave, using the same route and trails that they used when they came. She cried as she stood there watching them, for she knew they had devoured tons of hay that night and they may be back soon for more.

The shingles soon left Daddy, but the rheumatism seemed to get worse for a few days.

"I've got to sit up for awhile," he coaxed one night. "Move that chair over here by my big leather one and I'll rest my leg on it and see if the darn thing will quit aching." Mama did as she was commanded, and padded the kitchen chair with a quilt. "Nope, nope. Move the quilt quick, It's too high!" She removed the quilt and started to put his leg back in position on the chair. "Oh no! I can't stand this either. Get me back in bed quick!"

While lying there, he thought out a solution. "I know Berla. Get the meat saw and take three inches off each leg on that chair. I think it will be just right then."

We watched Mama saw. Erma stood the closest and swayed back and forth in rhythm with each stroke. Finally she commenced singing. "Saw my leg off, saw my leg off, saw my leg off, and throw the piece away." We adopted this little song, added it to the rest of our childish songs, and sang it for years.

The little chair did the trick. We could hold Daddy down no longer.

Daddy detested being a "gummer." As soon as he was able, he went to town, got on the stage that went to Idaho, and found a dentist to make him a set of teeth. He was gone five days, but Hazel, sturdy, stout, and used to the winter winds, took over like a man. She had been born and reared on a ranch, rode with cattle all summer on the range, and braved the cold blasts of winters while helping her father feed cattle.

We loved Hazel, and I would sit and look at her and wish she were my big sister so her name could be Chambers instead of Hedrick, then she could live on and on with us.

Mama called Margaret, Erma and me to her side one night. She sat close to the table and had the mail order catalog under the light of Carrie. "Children, it is time for the spring thaws. Your overshoes are nearly gone. Hazel is going to return to her home soon and won't be able to take you to school much longer, so I wondered if you would like to have a pair of these little boots. You can wade in the water with them on, up to your knees and not get wet."

We were so elated we could hardly believe it. We had never had a pair of boots in our lives. Mama said we could get them in either red or black. Of course, we chose the pretty bright color.

Before school finished that spring, Daddy felt fine, and Mr. Hedrick needed Hazel on the range. We girls and Mama shed a few tears, and Daddy stood with bowed head, as we stood in the yard and waved to Hazel as she rode away on Nancy, leading Clipper.

Chapter XVI
A BREAK WITH THE ICE

We could feel spring in the air again. Mama had been saving eggs for quite a while. She carefully packed them in sawdust around blocks of ice to keep them fresh. Daddy cheerfully said one morning, "Today would be a good day to go to town and dispose of the eggs. I think I should go while I can still travel with Sleigh-Bob. Would you and the children like to go with me?"

Mama had been up most of the night with little Clifford who had had an earache. "I would love to go, but it wouldn't be wise to take the baby out, so I'll stay home with the boys and you take the girls.

Today was Saturday and we didn't have to go to school. We were pleased with the opportunity.

"Well, come then girls," he said. "Let's go to the ice house and get the eggs." We dug carefully for a long time before we were sure we had them all. We likened it to an Easter egg hunt, but thought it was even more fun. As we left, we kissed Mama and our little brothers, and were off on a happy adventure.

When we got to Goe's, Daddy stopped to see if he could bring them anything from town. We asked Louise if she wanted to go with us and, of course, she did. Mrs. Goe asked Daddy if I could come back and stay with Louise all night as they had been invited to go with Bill McInelly to an old folks dance up in the country, and Louise would be left alone as Florence, Benny, Lyle, Bill and Byron were going on a sleigh-riding party with some of the older children of the flats.

Upon arriving in town, about noon, we saw many men gathered on the steps of the little brick store. Daddy could hardly wait to get his team tied to the post so he could get into the conversation. He recognized this as being the annual betting day for the ice going out on Jackson's Lake. He was happy he chose this day, the day of the betting, to go to town. Daddy wasn't a gambler, but he did like to make a bet once in a while. No certain day was set aside for such, but anytime after the first of April, whenever enough men got together and started a discussion going about it, the betting began.

Those who had actually witnessed the event in the past years described the ice moving out of the lake as being one of the most spectacular things they had ever seen.

We could tell right straight this could be a hot and heavy argument. One man stood waving his arms in the air and saying, "I tell you, I remember because—

Someone jumped into the conversation then and said, "It wasn't that day at all. It must have been the first day of May. I remember because—"

"No, no, you are both wrong," another one said. "I remember my wife being in the hospital with a new baby last year on the first and I was with her, and I know that wasn't the day."

Another man voiced in, "It was the fourteenth of May it went out last year, and the eleventh the year before. I was the winner last year. I'll never forget it. I stood on the bank of the lake for a week, expecting it to go. The weather had suddenly taken a change. On the fourteenth of May at 12:30, the wind came up and a warm Chinook moved in. I could see the water rising gradually above the ice, and shifted and churned. By four o'clock, it was floatin' with speed. It made me dizzy to watch it."

One man after the other picked up the conversation from there. It got so loud and rowdy that no one could hear the words of another.

Daddy could stand it no longer. "Listen fellows! Every one of you listen to me a minute! No use of us standin' here arguin.' Let's get the bet going about it."

From the crowd, a man stepped forward who lived on the shore of Jackson's Lake, and said, "I have lived there for about fourteen years, and I have watched the ice go out every time. It has never gone on the same day of the year yet. Anyone's guess is as good as the next one's. I'll hold the stakes boys," he said in a joking manner.

One man shouted, "Let him hold them. He is the perfect man to hold stakes, because he lives there and he will know the exact date."

"All right, how much do you want to bet?" the man from the Lake asked.

One man drew out a dollar bill and waved it in the air and said, "Let's make it a dollar apiece this year."

Another man drew forth a five dollar bill and said, "I'll raise you four and make it five." They argued for a moment then agreed that five dollars it would be.

The man from the Lake took a little notebook from his shirt pocket and wrote the bets down.

Jim Deloney . . . . . $5.00 . . . . . April 30th at 2 p.m.
Walter Spicer . . . . $5.00 . . . . . May 3rd at 4 p.m.
Fred Lovejoy . . . . $5.00 . . . . . May 20th at 4 p.m.
Si Ferrin . . . . $5.00 . . . . . May 10th at 3 p.m.
C.H. Brown . . . . . $5.00 . . . . . April 29th at 1 p.m.
J.R. Jones . . . . $5.00 . . . . . May 2nd at 5 a.m.
Bill Giles . . . . $5.00 . . . . . May 14th at 3 p.m.

"Hold everything!," Daddy shouted. "I've got to see if the storekeeper will buy my eggs before I can bet." Everyone laughed and decided to give him ten minutes to make the transaction.

Daddy felt this was his lucky day. He got eighty cents a dozen for Mama's eggs. The store clerk told him these were the first eggs they had seen in several weeks.

Daddy ran back to the circle of men and placed his bet.

Jim Chambers........$5.00..........May 8th at 3 p.m.

Only one man backed out of the crowd without betting.

The other sixteen men each forked over five dollars, leaning over the notebook as the man taking the stakes marked his name down, making sure the exact time of month and hour of day were properly placed beside his name.

"Now, said the man from the Lake, "I will be as honest as Abe about this thing and the very day and hour it goes out, I'll make a personal trip to town to pay off the winner."

"Fair enough, fair enough!," each shouted as he went on about his business.

Daddy took us back into the store and bought us each an apple. He came out with a big box of groceries and the change left from the twenty five dollars and sixty cents he received for the thirty two dozen eggs, after the five dollars was taken out.

On our way home, I said to Daddy, "Daddy, I was afraid for a few minutes—"

"Afraid of what honey?" he asked.

"Afraid those men were going to get in a fight."

Daddy laughed and said, "No, honey. Men just like to holler around when they get together. It is their nature to act like that."

"How much money are you taking home to Mama?" I asked.

"Oh, enough to cheer her," Daddy replied.

When we got back to Goe's, Daddy asked me if I wanted to stay all night with Louise. That pleased both her and me, but I didn't know if Mama would approve of it or not. I remembered the time after school one night Louise and I decided between us that I should go to her house and stay all night, and without debating, I went. When my sisters got home without me, my Mama was very disturbed for my not having her permission first. But if Daddy said I could stay this time, I was willing.

When Mr. and Mrs. Goe kissed us good-bye, they told us to go to bed early and asked what we would like for them to bring home as a surprise. Louise said, "A lollypop."

After they were gone, I asked Louise, "What is a lollypop?"

"Oh, it's a great big candy sucker," she said, showing me with her hands how big. "Big enough to last all one day."

The next morning when we awoke, we each had a lollypop on our pillow.

While Mr. and Mrs. Goe were gone, it started to rain. We had just gone to bed and all at once a stream of water hit us in the face. The roof was leaking. I could tell they were prepared for such a thing though, as Louise got a lot of buckets and started placing them around in the room in the likely places the water would come through. I thought this great fun to lay there and listen to the rain splash in the buckets. The next day, when I got home, I said to Mama, "I wish we had a house like Goe's, so it would leak and we could put buckets around to catch the rain." Then I asked her, "What did you think about Daddy betting on the ice?"

"Betting on the ice!" she said in astonishment.

Daddy had warned the other girls not to mention it to Mama for fear she wouldn't like him spending her egg money that way, but had forgotten to tell me. This opened a barrage of question, quite justifiable. One must have known Mama to feel what was in her heart that day.

The thaws came, but we were ready for them. We had been coaxing Mama for more than a week to let us take our panty-waists and long-legged underwear off, but she said, "May the first is soon enough for that, my dears. You know if you take your warm clothes off any sooner, you may catch a cold, and that means a lot of doctoring, caster oil, staying inside, and even missing school, so we had better leave them on a few more days."

We would do anything to avoid the caster oil, a remedy for everything.

Never did happier children ever live than were we the

morning we waded to school for the first time in our new boots. Mama cautioned us not to wade in deep water. The sound of nature was all around us with water running in gullies, Meadowlarks singing, and squirrels chirping. That morning's walk refreshed and invigorated us. Those little red boots pulled us to the mud puddles like magnets pull iron. We waded in mud, ankle-deep, looking behind us as we pulled our boots from the squishy mire, to see which one left the deepest tracks. The next stream of water we came to, we washed our boots clean.

We were the envy of every child in school that day. Louise traded me her new pencil for a turn in my boots at recess. I stood my boots in the front of the room, facing me where I could keep an eye on them all day.

At noon, I tried to eat my lunch, but my head was bursting with pain. That afternoon, I had a stuffy feeling in my head, I told Mrs. Saunders I could smell blood. So sure I was catching cold, she blamed it onto my new boots not being high enough. She felt my feet and they were damp, but I tried to tell her I hurt in my head and not in my feet.

All the rest of the students went out to play for afternoon recess. I hung my head on my desk. I felt dizzy. My head felt as if it were a big, blown-up balloon. I thought, "Oh, oh, here comes a dose of caster oil for me." Louise borrowed my boots again.

All at once, I felt something hot hit my face. I raised my head and put my hand to my nose. Blood was spirting from both nostrils, dripping on my desk and down my dress. Mrs. Saunders wrung a towel out of cold water, slapped it to my face, then wrung out another one and put it to the back of my neck. In seconds, the one to my face was covered with blood. She had no way to get help, and knew I would weaken fast. She folded a piece of heavy, white drawing paper and fitted it under my top lip. This acted as a tourniquet, stopping the blood. She kept me there on her bed for an hour, then dismissed school early, gave Margaret two clean wet towels and three wet dishtowels and instructed us to go straight home. She said, "Bertha, don't you stop to wade in the water with your new boots, or you may never make it." She promised to watch us until we got out of sight. Before we went down in the swale where she could no longer see us, we waved to her to let her know I was all right. She waved back to us.

I felt quite well until we got about halfway home and my nose started bleeding again. I held it tight and used the towels over my face. This frightening me, I started running, causing the blood to spirt faster. Margaret rinsed the towels out in every creek we passed. She seemed more frightened than I.

When we got home and saw a strange horse tied to the fence in our yard, we were more excited than ever. We knew we had company.

When we opened the door, we all asked in unison, "Who is here? Whose horse is that outside?"

Mama took one look at me and nearly fainted, and ran for Cure All For All. She read all about the symptoms of nosebleeds, treatments and the cause.

About an hour before we got home, Mama's brother, Frank Stevens, had ridden up on a horse. He lived in Idaho and a man there had hired him to take a band of horses over the Tetons, into Jackson, Wyoming. He was a real cowboy. The kind who wears chaps, cowboy hat and boots. He had ridden since early morning, and enjoyed the fresh cantor in the cool, spring air, until he came to the Snake River. There wasn't a bridge over the river, but a Ferryboat instead. He couldn't drive the horses onto the Ferry. He used his long quirt, but they refused to jump onto it. The red stallion which had led the band the entire way gave a plunge into the river. The rest followed him. Uncle Frank watched the horses while they swam across the cold, swift current, and wondered if they made it, could the horse he was riding swim it with him on its back. It wasn't difficult for the others, and one by one they reached shore, climbed the bank, shook themselves and appeared to be refreshed.

"I wonder what to do," he thought.

The Snake, high and roily, churning more turbulantly than he had ever seen it, looked wicked this morning. There was no one at the Ferry to help him, and when his horse saw the others make the plunge, he became anxious to follow. Uncle Frank knew he would get the saddle wet and probably his legs, and chaps, but he made the only decision to be made. He gave his horse a little rein and a tap with his spurs. They were doing quite well, with Uncle Frank still straddling the horse, holding his feet high on top of its neck, when all at once they entered a whirlpool. Down and around they went, completely submerged. He knew they would both drown if he tried to stay on. He thought if he gave a big spring from the horse's back he could out-leap the whirlpool, but as he stood up in the saddle to make the dive, his feet were wet and they went out from under him, and he fell in the middle of the fast, whirling water. He knew the weight of the horse's body would make the suction greater and drag him under, and he wouldn't have a chance. Around he kept going, until the undercurrent pulled him downstream. He tried to relieve himself of his chaps, but couldn't get them unbuckled. With his life nearly gone, he felt something go past him, and saw it was his horse. He grabbed its tail. They were both out of the whirlpool by now and headed for the shore, but Uncle Frank, too weak to even try to swim, just held on, using all the strength he had. Just before they reached the bank, Uncle Frank let loose, knowing he may get both hind feet in his face if he didn't.

The horse climbed the bank and started off to catch the others. Uncle Frank hollered, "Whoa! Whoa!" The animal obeyed his command, dripping wet, and trembling, and every muscle in his body twitching.

Uncle Frank dragged his soaked body out of the water, crawled over to his horse on his hands and knees, took the reins in his hands and laid down on the green, upholstered bank and started breathing heavily. He felt for his glasses and they were gone. Really sick, he commenced to heave. He had swallowed so much of that muddy water, he felt as if he had taken in half of the Snake River.

Still shaking two and a half hours later, he and his horse reached Poverty Flats.

I curiously made my way to the bedroom door, weak and tired, and saw Uncle Frank stretched out on Mama's and Daddy's bed. I managed a disappointed smile. I knew neither he nor I felt like having the good old tussling match we always had when he came to see us. He was one of my favorite people, my long beloved uncle, and whenever he came he would pick me up in his arms, throw me into the air, shake me on my way down and the scuffling match would be on. But we were both quite content with a little hug that night.

On the eighth day of May, Daddy said to Mama as he dressed, "Well, this is my lucky day. Today I'll get word that the ice is going out on the lake."

Mama had nearly forgotten how upset she had been over Daddy's gambling act, but this reminded her to be perturbed again. "Huh!" she replied. "What do you think you are, psychic or something? That is so much water under the bridge now. Let's forget it."

"So much ice, my dear," Daddy chuckled, then tried to kiss her, but she pushed him aside.

The day went on and by night, Mama reminded him, "Guess you are satisfied now that you didn't win, and remember I told you so."

The next day, about ten o'clock, a man came riding up on horseback.

"Who in the world can this be coming?" Mama asked as she saw him about a half-mile away. He was a stranger to all of us. Daddy wasn't at the house at the moment. Mama waited until he knocked on the door before she opened it. He greeted her and handed her an envelope.

"Oh dear, this must be serious!" she said, expecting it to be a telegram. She took it from the man and ripped the envelope open and read—

"This is to inform you that you are the winner, Jim. Ice went out May 8th at 4 p.m." In the envelope were eighty dollars in greenbacks. Mama went to the cupboard and took two dollars from Rainy Day, to tip the man, then thanked him for bringing the message, but he refused, saying he could not take the money.

"I am performing my duty as I promised."

"Then will you come in for a hot cup of cocoa and a cookie?" Mama asked.

"No, thank you. I must be on my way. Congratulate Jim for me, will you?" Then, tipping his hat, he closed the door behind him.

When Daddy came, Mama said to him, "Sir Hon, you did pretty well. I'll split the dividends with you."

This little bit of money was a flashing signal to Mama. She wouldn't admit it, but she too had a small streak of speculation within her. She called it conservativeness, and good judgment. Already planning on how she too could have a day of glory. "One day—one day of glory, is all I hope for in my life," she thought. "I must speculate on something. I know!" Then she clicked her tongue, and said, "I'm going to set hens, I'm going into the chicken business in a big way."

Before long, she had setting hens all over the place, under little separate, slab coops, in bushel baskets, and in the strawstack. She set twenty eight hens with thirteen and fourteen eggs each. She figured this would give her approximately four hundred new chickens and with half average of hens and cocks, she would keep the females and sell the males. She laughed as she figured her income one night and said, "Maybe, if I can keep selling eggs at eighty cents a dozen, I'll change the name of this ranch from Poverty Flats to Prosperity Palace."

Mama worked hard all summer and did raise a big flock of chickens. And now, what had once been a pastime, turned into a big project, just as she had wanted it. By late fall, the pullets were producing. She got thirty five cents a dozen for the small eggs and fifty cents a dozen for the large ones. Mama knew she was deeply engaged in supplying the town's appetite with a prized necessity. Her project worked each of us harder. The boys gathered eggs three times a day. We girls had the unwanted job of washing eggs, wrapping each one with a page from the old mail order catalog, or packing it in sawdust. Daddy, forced to take them to market at least once a week, said, "Between coop and market, the egg is a lasting nuisance."

Daddy entered the store one day to sell the eggs. People were crowding in the store to purchase tickets. Daddy inquired about what was going on. He learned that an elderly native of town had taken a lot of pictures of wild animals, invented a machine with which to show them on a wall, and now was ready to have his grand opening.

"When does this show begin, and how much are the tickets?" Daddy asked.

"It starts tomorrow night, in the Club House at eight o'clock, and the tickets are fifty cents for adults and twenty-five cents for children," the old man's son, Lester, replied. "Would you like some Mr. Chambers?" the lad inquired.

Daddy remembered one other time he spent Mama's egg money, and decided to talk the matter over with her first. "Maybe tomorrow son, but right now I've got to be gettin' along home."

142

When Daddy told us there was going to be a show in town, Mama asked, "A theater show? A real theater, and pictures of real live animals? We'll be there." And, turning to us children, she said, "The first picture show you will have ever seen."

Every family in the town was represented. Ladies came with their fancy hats on. Men put on suits and ties. I had never seen so many people in one place before in my life. For seats, blocks of wood with planks across were placed in rows in the Club House.

As Mr. Leek showed his pictures on the wall, he had a rhythmic story he related in a drawling voice, to go with each one. He told of the elk herds and called them WAPITI.

"The Wapiti with antlers wide—
Roaming o'er the mountain side—
The bull-elk sounding bugle calls—
Echoes through the canyon walls.
    Turn the crank, Lester, turn the crank!
The coyote howling at the moon—
Tells us that winter's coming soon—
His playful mate is at his side—
Running o'er the country wide.
    Turn the crank, Lester, turn the crank!
The western hare with fur so white—
Trailing over drifts at night—
Feeding from the farmer's hay—
And making for the owl, his prey.
    Turn the crank, Lester, turn the crank!"

Verse after verse went on about the tree squirrels, fish, badger, deer, bear, and all the native animals around Jackson Hole.

In the midnight hours, as we returned home, Mama rejoiced. "Well worth the price of admission." This was a happy day. Things did look more prosperous to her. She had doubled her money in Rainy Day since she put the forty

143

dollars there from the bet—and a new theater in town—
"maybe there will be one day of glory in my life somewhere
yet," she said.

Chapter XVII
WORTH A SHILLING

Mama loved the month of May. She said it always gave her the feeling of resurrection to see the Buttercups, Johnny-Jump-Ups, Rooster Heads, and Crocuses in full bloom and smell their sweet fragrance which filled the air. The Grandpa Whiskers, with their sleepy, tall, tousled heads, were about the only flower which appeared to be "not quite ready for spring."

Standing in the open doorway of the bedroom, she gazed at the Tetons, still crowned with glaciers, but their foothills bursting with fresh, foliage—soft, and green. Even the frogs crawled out of their hibernation places under the frozen banks, and croaked happily in May.

We girls weren't so happy over May, except that the long-handled underwear could now come off. The days were getting longer, and we wanted to play out late, but when the frogs croaked at night, this was signal enough for Daddy to know he had put in a full day's work and he wanted to go to bed. So we were called in then, as he couldn't sleep while we children were making a noise. He believed in the old adage, "Early to bed, and early to rise."

"I hate to stay inside and bake bread and iron on a beautiful day such as this," Mama said. "I would much rather be out in the dirt digging and planting flowers. Right now, I wish I had time to loiter near the swamps to listen to the red-winged Blackbirds sing as they sway to and fro on the long-stemmed cattails, or to walk in the highlands and hear the Meadowlarks sing, 'A Meadowlark is a pretty little bird,' but I don't have time, and I must go cheerfully along." (A statement Mama used often). "Bertha, I'm going to skim the cream off two more pans of milk and then there will be enough for one more churning. Will you start that while I mix bread?"

145

I loved hot bread with freshly churned butter, so I commenced my task enthusiastically, singing, "Around the churn this cream goes, but when it turns to butter nobody knows."

Daddy had been working outside all day. About one thirty he drove up with Dan and Bally, close to the house and shouted to Mama, "Babs, come here!"

Mama was putting the bread in the tins. She rolled the dough from her hands the best she could, and went to the door.

"Put your jacket on and come help me!" he said. When Daddy decided to do something, it had to be done right now. Not that he was impatient, but rather, ambitious.

"I can't go anywhere with you now, Jim," said Mama. "I'm putting bread in the tins and I'll have to stay with if for an hour and a half. What do you want me to do?"

"I'm ready to sow wheat and if I can get you to drive the team, I can finish it in one day."

"Well, you will have to wait awhile, but I'll put the bread on the warming oven to hurry it along, and will be with you as soon as I can," she promised.

"I'm in a terrible hurry," he mused aloud. Then he took Tiny Tin, which was hanging on the outside of the house, and threw it in Lumber Wagon. "And Babs, I'd like to—" His words were lost as he grabbed Dan by the bit and led the horses to the granary where he filled Tiny Tin with wheat. It was the same round, tin tub we all used for our Saturday night baths. He placed it at the back of Lumber Wagon, tied his horses to the fence, then ran to the potato bin and sprouted potatoes while the bread baked. One thing Daddy couldn't stand to do was to waste a manhour.

Mama climbed up on Lumber Wagon and six little shadows followed her. She took the lines in her hands. We children sat in a semi-circle between her and Tiny Tin, while Daddy knelt down at the back of the wagon with both hands in the wheat.

"Now drive slowly!" Daddy cautioned. "And when you get to the bottom of the field, swing wide so I won't sow the same patch twice." Mama had been in this same driver's seat before, but Daddy had to offer so much advice.

He put his right hand in the wheat, grabbed a handful, flung it over his left shoulder, then a handful in his left hand and flung it over his right shoulder. We children offered to help, but Daddy was afraid if we did, he might have a few stocks of wheat come up in a crooked line, so we were only along for the ride.

About the third time around we children were begging to get off. We would rather play than just sit and jolt. We had to stay with it though until Daddy ran out of wheat and had to go to the granary for more.

Just as Daddy and Mama had finished sowing the grain, a soft, warm, spring rain fell. We children were delighted with the haloes of rainbows over Sheep Mountain.

"Yep," said Daddy, "that rainbow is promising me, not just one bucket of gold, but many. In the fall, when this wheat all turns brown, every bucketful will be worth that much gold."

That night, with pencil and paper, Daddy figured the acres he had sowed and about how many bushels of wheat he could get to the acre.

"Berla, if this crop turns out as good as I think it will, we can lay in a good supply of groceries this fall and buy you and the kids some new winter clothes."

"It sounds exciting," said Mama, "but let's see the wheat in the sacks before I make out the order, huh?"

It wasn't long before the wheat sprouted. Daddy watered and cared for it tenderly, and every day he walked out in the field to measure a stock to see if it had grown any during the night.

It was Daddy's habit to be up early. Nearly every

morning, he scuffed his feet through the dew on the grass when he went to the field.

One morning before sun-up, he dressed and carefully slipped out of the house without awakening any of us. He heard a chirping sound and saw a beautiful, big tree squirrel, with bushy tail and yellow belly, running on the top rail of the pole fence around our yard. He went back to the house and got some bread and carefully placed it on the top rail, next to the buckpost, then stepped back and watched the squirrel come to it. The alert little animal took it in his two front paws and ate it while standing erect on his two hind legs. This went on morning after morning and the little fellow became so tame he ate out of Daddy's hands.

He forgot to tell Mama about it. She slept soundly while the feeding hour was going on, and squirrel had vanished by the time we all got up. But one morning Mama couldn't sleep so got up real early to feed her chickens, and there was squirrel running on the fence looking for his morsels. Mama got Meat-in-the-pot, and there wasn't enough left of squirrel to find the pieces. When Daddy came in for breakfast, she met him with "Guess what?" All excited, she didn't give Daddy time to guess anything. "I killed a weasel this morning. I'm glad I got up just when I did or he would have been in the coop after my chickens."

"Where did you shoot this weasel?," Daddy asked.

"Right out there on the top pole of the fence," Mama said, pointing to the exact spot.

Daddy put his face in his hands and shuddered. "It's all my fault," he said, "for not telling you. That was my pet squirrel. I have had him feeding right out of my hand."

By the end of July, Daddy came in the house one day with a long stock of wheat in his hand. "Just look at this sample of my wheat crop, Berla. We are going to have a bumper crop this year.

Mama examined the stock, still green, but a big head

was developing into the boot. "Well, Jim, I hope it is good. You have worked so hard for it."

"I have about two more months of hard work left with it, but I think my efforts will pay off." Daddy tipped his head and clicked his tongue. "In the not too distant future, we may even be able to build on a room to this house to make space for our growing family."

He had a fair crop of hay that year, but it wasn't as good as usual, for he had been devoting most of his time to the wheat crop, giving it most of the irrigation water.

One day, Daddy started off across the field riding old Doll with his shovel across his shoulder. Using his legs, he tried to kick Doll enough to make her travel just a little faster. He wasn't making progress fast enough so he used the reins to strap her. Finally he had her galloping at a good speed, but it still didn't suit him. He flapped his arms as if they were wings. "Whoa! Whoa!" He brought old Doll to a sudden halt, dropped the reins in front of her, jumped to the ground and ran across the fields with his shovel. He had to make use of every precious moment.

About as proud of her chickens as was Daddy of his wheat, Mama said one evening as she came from the coop with an apron full of eggs: "It is going to take a bumper crop of wheat this year to feed my chickens. Sir Hon, look at that box full of eggs, will you?"

Daddy peered over the edge of the box and replied, "Why it was only five days ago that I took eggs to town and here I have to go with them again."

"I'll have them wrapped soon. We won't be going with them before tomorrow will we?" Mama asked in a joking voice as it was already getting dusk.

"No, tomorrow will be soon enough," Daddy joked back. "I'll get some binding twine while I'm in town. I'll need a lot of that this year for my wheat."

On his way to town, Daddy stopped at every neighbor's

house to tell his friends about his wheat crop.

"You lucky character, " said Mr. Goe. "You will be so rich, Jim, that you won't speak to us."

Jokingly, Daddy replied, "You can't tell a thing about me, Ben. Rich people usually get high hat all right."

Daddy went on his merry way, singing, whistling, and planning. He was still happy on his way home. He had bought a lot of groceries. Eggs were now selling for sixty cents a dozen. Mama was happy with his purchases and the extra money. She hummed a little tune as she took Rainy Day from the shelf.

The next day, about all the ranchers on Flat Creek rode up to see if Daddy had stretched the truth about his wheat crop.

Bill McInelly said he had never in all his life seen such a stand of wheat. Each man offered to help Daddy harvest his crop when ready. "I'll be the first one here," said Bill.

"I'll be the second one," chimed Mr. Van Leerdam.

"Just shout when ready, and I'll sure be glad to help harvest it, Jim," spoke Johnny Infinger.

"I'll probably have to have a lot of help, so I'll remember this and thanks a lot," Daddy said.

By the end of September, Daddy had enlarged his grain bin by taking the partition out and using the tool shed and granary as one big storage space. The tools were taken to the barn and hung up on nails and stored overhead, above the rafters.

"One more week Babs, and we'll have a threshing crew to feed. It may take us several days, so you had better get some baking done ahead." Daddy seemed a lot more anxious for that crew of men to come than was Mama.

The next few days were hot ones, and the grain ripened fast. "How many days left now, Jim, before the crew of men will be here?" Mama asked.

"Three," Daddy replied. "That is, if it doesn't storm and

stop us. It has been so hot that I wouldn't doubt if it rained before long."

That afternoon, Daddy was in the field and working so hard, when he noticed a big, black cloud overhead. It had a white underlining all the way around it. Daddy headed for the house and had to run to beat the storm.

"Here it comes Berla, here it comes! The ruination of us," he said, fairly crying.

Within seconds, a terrific storm hit and it was HAIL. It beat down on the roof so loudly Daddy and Mama could hardly hear each other. They stood in the kitchen door and watched pellets come down as big as marbles. They watched the ground turn white. A terrible thunderstorm accompanied the hail.

Daddy sat mournfully on a chair. Mama tried to comfort him, but he knew once more he had been ruined.

When the storm passed over, Daddy walked slowly, head bowed, one foot dragging behind the other one, to what had been a field of fortune. He returned to the house, flung his weary body on the bed and cried for half an hour.

"Did it take the whole crop, Jim?," Mama asked as timidly as she knew how.

"Every kernel dear, every kernel. It is shelled out on the ground, heads broken off and only the stock is standing."

"Let's sell out and move somewhere else," Mama offered as a consoling suggestion.

"Sell for WHAT?," Daddy muttered in a voice trembling with emotion. "This place is ONLY WORTH A SHILLING."

Chapter XVIII
PRESTON

Arriving in the mail one day, a letter came to Daddy from his cousin in Utah. He wanted to get away from the city and spend a summer with us. He stated he would be happy to work for his room and board.

"I'll let him help me build the new barn," Daddy said, as he wrote Preston and told him to come right away. He thought if he couldn't depend on the weather, he had a better chance to raise hay than wheat, so decided to buy a few head of cows and go into the cattle business.

We didn't know exactly when Preston would arrive, but Slumber Tuff was brought in and set up in the kitchen again.

He arrived in Jackson on the stage and had no way of letting us know he was there, so walked all the way from town. He reached Poverty Flats just before dark, with enough enthusiasm to spread all over Flat Creek. So engrossed with our beautiful country, he said he felt happy to be alive, to feel these rich moments, and could hardly wait to get started in the timber.

"The first thing to be done," Daddy explained to Preston, "is to hook Dan and Bally to a slip scraper and clear the piece of sagebrush ground where the barn is to be built." Daddy gave Preston a few lessons on how to harness and unharness a horse.

Preston knew so many exciting stories about the city we children followed him all day, begging for another one. He never seemed to tire of us, nor the stories. I revered him as a Prince right out of Fairy Land.

We begged to go to the timber with the men, for they were working just beyond the picnic grounds, but Daddy said it would be too dangerous to go while they were felling trees, but promised we could when it was time to haul them out.

The time came when Daddy said we could go tomorrow if we would retire to bed early and get a good night's sleep. Mama said she would pack a picnic and go with us, because Uncle Andy and Aunt Ida were to come through Dry Hallow and meet us there.

I had a frustrated feeling all night of time standing still and the anxiety of my mind wouldn't permit me to sleep. Preston had told us he had a special story he saved to tell this day, and my curiosity, together with the anxiety, was almost more than I could stand.

Daddy put some flatboards on the wagon so we had a place to ride. We didn't seem to notice the rough spots in the road that day. And in all the picnics we had ever attended on those picnic grounds, this one topped them all.

Trimming the branches and peeling the thick bark from the fallen trees, the three men worked hard all day. We had fun watching them for awhile, but Mama asked us to stay with her and Aunt Ida at the picnic grounds most of the time so they could keep an eye on all of us at once.

We had great fun feeding the pine-squirrels, which paraded before us for hours. We threw them bits of sandwiches, cake and potato salad, and watched them fumble each little morsel in their front paws, stick it in their jaws and then run up a tree, out on a limb, and store it for future food. Down the tree one would come again for another bite. Little brothers giggled and played with them most of the day.

It was getting late in the afternoon when Daddy noticed a big, black cloud over the Grand Teton. "We've got to get this load on quick, and get out of here boys, because when a storm comes up this way from the Tetons, and meets up with the downwind from Flat Creek canyon, it usually is a dilly," Daddy said, as he heaved one end of a big tree to the bolster of the wagon.

Mama and Aunt Ida had noticed the cloud too. Mama

153

said, "Come girls, help me gather up the picnic things, and Bertha, you go tell Daddy it looks as if a big storm is coming so he had better hurry."

I ran as fast as my two short legs could carry me. When I told Daddy that Mama thought we should go, he said, "I think so too honey, and we'll put just enough more logs on this load so we will have a place to ride, then we will be out of here. Tell Mama we'll be there in ten minutes." I ran all the way back to the picnic grounds. The ladies and the girls had everything in neat order.

Both wagons left the canyon at once. Uncle Andy and Aunt Ida went back the way they came, and we headed out in the opposite direction.

As we left, Daddy could see I had tears in my eyes. I always cried when it stormed, for I was equipped with sensitive feelings. He said, "Preston, tell another story!"

We had gone only about a mile when the heavens opened. Mama huddled us all close together and put the quilt, which she had taken to spread on the ground for the picnic, over our heads. I felt so sorry for Daddy and Preston, for there wasn't room for them under the quilt. Somehow, though, I felt safer there in the dark where I couldn't see the storm.

Lightning and thundering now, each time a loud clap of thunder came, all of us children would flinch and moan. We remembered we had a cousin killed with lightning and knew there was no protection for us in that canyon.

Dan and Bally sensed the danger too. They were traveling as fast as Daddy allowed. The rain which had been coming down in torrents, suddenly stopped, but the lightning was still razor-sharp.

Then a tragic thing happened. The horses were stricken. Both fell to the ground. Daddy felt the shock go through his body, but he and Preston jumped to the horses' sides. We children screamed. I could feel Mama trembling, even though she tried to comfort us by saying, "Now dears, try to remain calm! The horses will be all right in a few minutes. They have been stunned by the lightning, that's all. Try not to be worried nor frightened. Be brave children! Be brave."

Another streak of lightning flashed before us and we saw white. The thunder shook our load. Daddy said, "Unhook Bally, Preston, and I'll unhook Dan. If ever they come to, they may struggle to get up and upset the wagon. Babs, you and the kids stay where you are, because you are as safe there as anywhere, and kids, be still! You can't help the matter by crying."

"Bally is going to be all right Jim," said Preston. "He's breathing heavily, but I think he will soon come out of it."

"I can't feel a sign of life coming from Dan," Daddy said. He straddled Dan's motionless body and pushed on his sides, trying to get him breathing again.

Bally groaned. His sides heaved in and out, his legs twitched. He raised his head as if to look around to see where he was, then sprang to his feet, shook the harness on his body, looked down at Dan and whinnied. Preston grabbed Bally by the bit and spoke kind words to him.

Taking Dan's two front feet, Daddy rolled him over on his back and said, "Dan is DEAD!"

Bally, quaking like the leaves on an Aspen tree, we knew he still didn't have full control of his muscles. He walked stiff-legged and stood over the body of his dead mate, head bowed with remorse.

"Well, I don't know what to do now," Daddy said. "But I'll have to go for help. Preston, if you stay here and watch Bally, I'll take the Missus and the children and go to Kelly's. Maybe they can stay there and I'll borrow a team from George and be back as soon as possible."

It was nearly dark when we left Preston alone. Within moments we were to stand face to face with the blackness of night. The mud, ankle deep, and slippery, made it almost impossible to stand up and keep traveling. Daddy took Earl in his arms and Mama carried Clifford. We three girls and Archie were on our own. We felt darkness trapping us, and stopped many times as we couldn't see where we were going. The lightning was a blessing to us now because it lighted our way, even though the storm had traveled beyond us.

We were wet, tired, cold, muddy, and hungry when we came to the end of our one and a half mile, muddy trek. Mrs. Kelly took us in, washed and fed us, and was better to us than kissin' kin.

Some quilts on the floor provided a sleeping place for Margaret and Erma. Mrs. Kelly took me to the bedroom, where her two little boys, Richard and Donald, were moved over, and I snuggled in between them. Archie, Earl and Clifford were wrapped in some dry blankets and put on Mrs. Kelly's bed.

Mr. Kelly and Daddy talked the situation over and decided to take his team, wagon and a lantern and go back to get Preston and Bally. They could see another storm coming. It wasn't unusual for one storm to follow another one, especially in the vicinity of the Tetons.

"We'll have to hurry," said Daddy, "or we'll be caught in another storm."

Due to the blackness of the night, it wasn't easy for even the horses to travel. A terrific wind came out of Flat Creek canyon. Trees were swaying and bending with the wind. Several big ones had fallen across the road, and Daddy and Mr. Kelly had to remove them before they could travel on.

Just before they reached the scene of the accident, it started lightning and thundering again.

"I thought so," said Daddy, "as I couldn't see any stars shinin' and I knew another storm would follow."

"One almost always follows another one out of this canyon, Jim," said Mr. Kelly. "I'll bet if it were light, we could see black clouds hanging over the Tetons, and you know that means another storm from that direction will meet this one out of Flat Creek and it will be another whopper."

A streak of lightning, a clap of thunder, and more torrents of rain came when the men were within shouting distance of Preston. Daddy started calling his name, and from force of habit, whistled his night tune.

They received no answer from Preston. They stopped beside the load of logs. Bally was standing tied to the wagon in a pathetic condition. Preston had removed his harness.

Daddy called Preston again and said, "I hope that crazy city dude didn't get frightened of the dark and start walking to meet us. If he did that, he surely got off on the wrong track."

Taking the lantern, Daddy looked under Lumber Wagon to see if Preston had crawled there for protection and had gone to sleep. The light reflected upon something. With the lantern in his hand, he went around Lumber Wagon and there saw Preston stretched out full length, lying on his back. Daddy knew he wasn't asleep. He said, "George, here he is, and something has happened to him." Daddy felt his heart leap. Never had he been so perplexed. Tragic? Yes, this was another fateful day in his life.

He lifted Preston to a sitting position, but his limp, unconscious body slumped over in Daddy's arms. Daddy could feel him breathing but his body felt cold. He knew Preston had also been struck by lightning. "That last close clap must have hit him, George. I don't think he has been here long."

Holding the lantern close, they could see the muscles in his face and neck twitch. They lifted him to Mr. Kelly's wagon and decided they had to travel much faster with him than stiff-legged Bally could keep up, so they left Bally tied to Lumber Wagon and headed for Kelly's house.

The lightning had worn itself out, but it was obvious that the rain would pour for hours.

The men each took his coat off and wrapped it around Preston. Daddy held his head in his lap while Mr. Kelly drove the team. Still unconscious when they arrived, Daddy and Mr. Kelly carried him to the house.

Mama and Mrs. Kelly were up waiting for them. They became all excited, as women do, when they saw the form of a stiff man.

The little ones were quickly removed from Mrs. Kelly's bed and put on the floor. The men undressed Preston while Mama and Mrs. Kelly went to work with towels wrung out of hot water. They saw his eyes open and roll back in his head. Then he opened his eyes and tried to focus them. One pupil much larger than the other one told them he was suffering from shock.

"Where am I?" were the first words he uttered.

"You are here in bed, and we are right with you and everything is going to be fine," Mama assured him, as she stroked his forehead. "Try not to be worried nor frightened and just sleep. We will stay right here."

Preston remembered her saying almost those exact words before, then recalled the lightning, we children crying, and Mama comforting us.

"I'm so sorry I caused you all this trouble. Whose house is this? Where are the children?"

Mama explained to him where he was, introduced Mr. and Mrs. Kelly, and told him we were safe, and sound asleep in bed.

"Thank God!" he said. "Thank God for that, and for good people." Then his eyelids closed again.

It was breaking dawn when Mr. Kelly saddled his horse for Daddy to ride to town for Dr. Huff.

We children awakened one by one, and were "hushed" and explained to that Preston was a sick man and he must have rest. I saw him lying there so still and I wondered if he would ever be able to tell us another story.

By noon, Daddy and Dr. Huff were back. Daddy tied the saddle horse to the back of the buggy and rode with the Doctor. Mama met them at the door, nodded, and winked her eye to let Daddy know Preston was doing as well as could be expected.

The Doctor had his little black bag with him again, which he took some medicine from, and gave to Preston and then said, "I must move him to the hospital, where I can keep a constant watch on him for several days. He is suffering from shock as well as burns."

Semi-conscious, Preston tried to help himself as they lifted him, wrapped in bedding, to the back seat of Dr. Huff's buggy. Mama offered to go along, but the Doctor said he would make it quite well. He knew Mama must be worn out from all the experience of the night, without any rest.

The two men went again for Bally, then took us home where we arrived thirty four hours after we had left home, happy and excited about going on a picnic. I don't know which was happier to see us; Fritz Yellowhair or unmilked Curley.

While lying in the hospital, Preston told the story how he thought he heard the men coming and he climbed upon the back wheel of Lumber Wagon to reach the top of the load where he thought he could see better, and a bolt of lightning struck so close to him the iron band of the wagon had made a perfect contact and he was the lightning's victim.

Daddy inquired from each of his neighbors if he had an extra horse he would sell, but no one had. Mr. McInelly offered to lend him a horse until he could buy one, but Daddy said he would find one or get along without.

One night, three weeks later, we had just finished our supper and were doing the dishes. Daddy and Preston were

159

discussing the fact that they had gone as far with the barn as they could, and now they had to do something about getting another horse. A knock came on the kitchen door. Daddy opened it and there stood John Kelly, an old cattle buyer. He talked in a high-pitched voice, wore chaps, leather coat, riding boots, and gloves. He carried a bedroll on the back of his saddle, and made the rounds often at the ranches on Flat Creek. He knew about the time of day each rancher sat down to eat. Without waiting for an invitation, he yanked his gloves off, threw his hat on the floor, pulled his chaps off, threw them in the corner, and poured some warm water from Copper-Topper, into the wash basin. Holding water in his cup-shaped hands, he blew as he washed his face up to his hair line. As he dried himself with the towel, he said, "Just a bowl of bread and milk Mrs. Chambers, just a bowl of bread and milk."

A bowl of bread and milk and some homemade jelly was about all we had left to offer him that night.

As soon as he had eaten his supper, he said, almost in one big breath, "I'll put my horse in your barn tonight Jim, and throw him a fork full of hay; then I'll be on my way in the morning. I knew you didn't have any cows to sell, but heard you were looking for a good horse. I think I know a man I can send up soon. He deals in horses all the time. Just give me a blanket Mrs. Chambers, or I'll bring my bedroll in, and I'll roll out here on the floor. One of you kids get me your dad's slippers. My feet are swollen from riding in these boots all day."

A horse trader came two days later. He had a beautiful pinto he was riding, and was leading three other horses. He didn't have a match for Bally, but Daddy said he would settle by buying a big, tall lanky sorrel mare he had if, when he came back in the country again, he would bring a match for Bally, and they could trade. The man agreed to take the mare back if he could do better for Daddy. Daddy went to the house to get the money to pay him. He lacked several dollars of having what the man wanted, so Mama emptied Rainy Day into her lap and counted out enough money to make the difference.

Daddy opened the mare's mouth. He remarked that her teeth showed she was still a young mare and he hoped she knew how to work.

The first time Daddy tried to put a harness on her, she stepped around and traveled in circles. Daddy finally got the harness on her back, but when he turned around to fasten it, she tried to take a bite out of Daddy's britches. Every time he tied her up, she would chew her rope in two. Mama named her "Big Bite."

Chapter XIX
SADDLING AN ELK

Mama awakened early one morning thinking about her new broom Daddy had brought from town the night before, so decided to get up and clean house before anyone got in her way. Upon arising, she discovered Daddy had slipped out without her knowing it. She dressed, put Copper-Topper on the stove to boil, then grabbed her new broom and commenced singing.

> "Happy is the farmer's wife
> Who sweeps with a new broom,
> And so with this invention
> I'll tidy up my room."

She then gathered up the dirt with a piece of pasteboard she used for a dust pan, put the sweepings in the stove, then stepped outside to replace the short, stubby, old broom, which hung upside down on the wall between two spike nails, with the new one. She met Daddy coming in with a bucket of steaming warm milk.

"Good morning Dear!" she exclaimed. "I want to thank you for buying me this new broom. You know the old saying goes, 'A new broom sweeps clean.' Well, I just swept all my cares away and burned them."

Daddy replied, "I wish I could get rid of my troubles that easy. This morning when I went to the barn to milk, I found seven head of elk in the barn with my cow. They had jumped through a window and had crowded Curley right down, stomping on her. Within a few minutes, she would have been dead. I had to get a stick and prod those darn things until I got them to jump back through the window. They were crowded against the door and I couldn't get it open."

Being early in the winter time, the elk were coming out of the deep snowclad mountains down to the farmer's stacks in an endless search for food, where the snow laid less deep

162

and food more plentiful. The big bulls soon learned how to use their antlers, with three prongs on the end, much like a pitchfork. A bull would reach over a haystack fence, plant his horns in the stack, and with a twist of his head, soon have a stack torn to pieces.

That night, while we children and Daddy slept peacefully, Mama heard a lot of stomping around the house. She got up and rattled the window with her fist, and in the moonlight saw several head of elk run away from the side of the house. She heard the howl of a coyote and soon many were yelping.

"What was all that noise about last night, Berla?" Daddy asked as he pulled his nightshirt over his head and dressed for the day.

"I didn't think you heard a thing," she answered. "You seemed to be sleeping so soundly." Then getting to her feet, she looked out the bedroom window and saw tracks everywhere. "Come here, Sir Hon! While you slept, I kept a vigilance on elk all night."

"I wonder if they're in the barn again." Then Daddy grabbed his heavy chore coat, overshoes, and cap and ran to the barn with a club.

Mama opened the door to reach for her new broom hanging on the outside wall and a gush of winter wind hit her in the face. Hanging onto the doorknob to keep the door from flying open with a bang, she saw her broom still hanging, but the straw all gone from it. The elk had eaten it during the night.

This was Sunday morning and Daddy announced to Mama that he thought he would ride over to pay Ershel Curtis a visit. "I'm going to see if he is being pestered too, or if I'm the only one in this neighborhood who is doing all the worrying and feeding." Daddy had taken about enough of this kind of destruction, and not only was he a man of many words, but a lot of action.

Ershel, about Daddy's age, had never married, still lived with his parents who were extremely religious and every Sunday went to church—rain, snow, sun or no.

When Daddy drove up, his friend Ershel was having a hard time trying to fix and rebuild fences around the stacks high enough and strong enough to keep these very breechy animals out.

"Jim," Ershel said, "what do you do to conquer these blasted elk? I have fed so many of them already this winter, I could feed twice the herd of cattle I'm feeding if I could keep these breechy beasts out of the stacks. They are so tame, or so starved, one or the other; they are coming out of the hills to the lowlands to feed with the cattle. My hard labors of all last summer aren't doing me much good. The elk are eating the hay faster than are the cattle."

"I know what you mean. I have been having trouble too." Then Daddy related the story about the elk jumping through the barn window, and the next night eating Mama's new broom.

"I don't doubt that a bit, Jim. Look at that big spike over there. He has been here so long he thinks he owns the place, therefore, he is a steady border. He is so tame I can't run him off with a pitchfork. I think he is tame enough to ride."

"Well, let's try him," Daddy suggested. "Open the barn door and I'll shoo him in."

"No, you open the barn door," said Ershel, "and I'll show you a sure way to get him." As usual, this day wasn't planned, it just happened.

Ershel took his pitchfork, flipped it in the edge of the haystack and pulled out a big pitchfork full of green hay, walked around the stack with it, passed the pet elk, and sure enough, he followed Ershel right into the barn. When Mr. Elk stuck his head in the manger to get the hay, Ershel closed the stanchion bar and they had him cornered.

"The next thing we have to do Ershel, is to get a saddle

on him." Both men were laughing, and wondering how to go about that. Ershel looked up and there hanging on the wall he saw his father's new saddle, the only one in the place that was handy at the moment. Mr. Elk was doing some high stepping, bucking and snorting, trying to free himself, but to no avail. Daddy carried more hay and finally the elk quieted down enough that they threw the saddle on him. This strange feeling thing, he didn't plan to go for, but pretty well tied, he couldn't do much about it. They fastened the saddle bellyband, and then got a halter around his nose with a rope for rein, discussing which one would climb into the saddle, and which one would lead him out, either position a dangerous one. Daddy took the rope in his hand while Ershel carefully released the stanchion bars, so as not to excite the elk.

"Getting into the saddle is the most important factor in the success of this game," said Ershel.

"Watch out for his horns!" Daddy warned.

"I will," Ershel replied. "To insure a good start, back him out and I'll grab the saddlehorn when you get him tied to the snubbin' post, and I'll fling on him so fast he won't have time to think."

Ershel had broken many a bronc and had ridden a time or two in the town frontiers, and had real confidence that he could ride that elk. Not so sure though he could guide him very well with only one rein said, "I think I'm ready." He knew he could jump or fall off any time he felt he had had enough.

Daddy anticipated holding the elk until Ershel climbed abroad, then all the rest would be up to Ershel. The elk backed out cautiously until he got to the door, then he leaped straight into the air and pulled Daddy out with him. Propelling arms and legs in the air, Daddy landed in the muck on his belly. Mr. Elk stopped for nothing. He jumped the corral fence and headed for the hills, with stirrups flying on both

165

sides.

"Well, I guess I'll not worry about that elk anymore," said Ershel. "He surely will never come back here anymore." Both men were laughing so hard they could hardly stand the feeling in their stomachs. A feeling one can only get at this point of laughter.

"Don't you think he'll ever come back to return the saddle?" Daddy asked while bent over holding his sides.

"The Saddle! Dad's new saddle!" It suddenly wasn't so funny to Ershel anymore. "How will we ever get that saddle back? Dad just traded a horse and thirty dollars besides, for that saddle. Oh, Jim, what will we do?"

Daddy tried to reason with Ershel that the elk couldn't go far with a saddle on it. Either he would get caught in some brush or trees with it on, and die, or another bull elk may even fight and kill him. Surely they could get the saddle!

They knew they would have to ride the hills hunting much harder and many times more often than ever before. To hunt elk and shoot one was fairly an easy task, but to hunt a special elk with a saddle on it was a different story.

Daddy left for home before long because he could see no use waiting any longer or he might be there when the old people got home from church, and besides that, Daddy needed some clean clothes. He assured Ershel he would keep an eye open all the time on trapping trips, and suggested that maybe the elk would come down some day to his place to feed.

About three days after this, Ershel's father discovered his saddle missing. He inquired of all his children and his wife if they had seen it, but no one had. Ershel didn't come right out and lie, but evaded the question by saying, "Where did you last have your saddle, father?" and "Somebody had to take that saddle off the hook. It just couldn't fall off and walk away."

After a week, the old man was sure someone had stolen

166

his saddle, so he went to town and put a notice of reward in the local newspaper.

When Daddy got home that afternoon, Mama could see he was in a MESS. "What happened to you, Sir Hon?," she asked in a puzzled voice, raising her eyebrows to look the situation over.

"Oh, I tried to help Ershel put a saddle on a wild critter," he replied, "and he was wilder than we figured him to be and he took off while I was trying to hold him long enough for Ershel to get into the saddle, and I wasn't man enough to do so. He pulled me a little way in the muck."

"A little way? It looks like a big way to me," Mama said. She didn't have any idea that this wild critter was an elk. "Did Ershel get hurt?"

"Nope, not at all. He just stood still and laughed at me," Daddy said.

In all the many years to come, so long as Ershel's father lived, Daddy nor Ershel told this story to one living soul, nor did they ever find the elk or hear of anyone killing one with a saddle on.

Mama never did guess why Daddy went hunting and trapping so often after this all happened.

Ershel finally consoled himself with, "It was cheaper to saddle him than feed him."

(P.S. The saddle was eventually found 50 years later by Jim Flower, the Foreman of the Elk Refuge, at the bottom of a steep canyon, nearly burried with mud and grass, and most of the leather pawed off by scavenging animals, and with a broken cinch, proving the elk wore it until he could cut the cinch with his hind leg. The saddle is now in the possession of the Author.)

Chapter XX
THE TUSK HUNTERS

For the past many years, Daddy had been hunting dead elk, but this episode made him hunt a little harder. He found many carcasses on the foothills, and always carried a pair of pliers with him for extracting the teeth. He felt lucky if he found one good pair in each head. Some were better than others, however, and bull elk have much better ivory than do cow elk.

Many a night Daddy would put a pan of coffee on the stove to brew, and after brewing slowly for a few hours, he would remove the solution from the stove, add a pinch of tobacco to it, giving it a golden brown color, then elk teeth were carefully dropped in and left to soak for twenty four hours. The next night he would put his overalls on with patches sewed over the knees, then sprinkle pumice on the patches, and rub the teeth in it for hours. We watched the whole process of soaking, rubbing, filing, and soaking again. When he got the exact shape, color, and shine on them, he sent them away to a company which bought them for jewelry. He would get from ten dollars to fifty for each pair, depending on the quality of the ivory. They always had to be sold in pairs.

Fortunately, Daddy found many elk soon after they had died. Stripping the dead animal of its valuable appendages, such as teeth, horns and hide, he was able to perform this task before malodor offended his nostrils. He tanned the hides, and sold them to the Indians who came each summer and camped close to us for about two weeks. They used them to make gloves and moccasins. Sometimes the Indians were poorer than Daddy. In this case, he would trade a hide for two pair of gloves. Of little value were the horns, except for decoration purposes in flower beds and along fence rails.

The granddad Indian of them all, named Nakoni Teoni, was the chief. His wrinkles reminded us of the crevasses in the mountains, and he talked just enough English with "heap big" added to everything, that Daddy could understand him well enough to barter with him.

Because of the elk, many changes were about to take place in the lives of the men who lived in this section of Wyoming.

Now being wiser about coming down in the winter to the ranchers' stacks to feed, they came in herds. One big bull would be in the lead and the rest following, wallowing through the drifts. They came in such quantities they had hard-beaten trails from the hills to the stacks. They weren't respective of fences, nor of man's property. They came like hobos, begging for a handout.

We awoke one morning to find a yard full of elk, browsing and pawing in the yard, trampling haystacks and mowing fences down. Daddy said, "Huh! They act as if they have come for a grand opening."

Just prior to this, the B.P.O.E. Lodge, whose nickname is "Elks," adopted the elk teeth as a part of their emblem jewelry. The men wore the elk teeth with pride. Ladies wore them in hat pins, rings, watch fobs, and cuff links. The elk had become an animal of renowned glory and they were acting as such.

Many strangers were seen in the little, peaceful, town of Jackson. they started coming in about the same time of year the elk came off the mountains. People were curious about so many strangers, but no one questioned why they were there.

Coming home one night after baiting his traps, Daddy said, "Berla, I was nearly killed today. A bullet passed right over my head, and an elk dropped dead within a few yards of me."

"Who do you think fired the shot?" Mama queried.

169

"I don't have the slightest idea," Daddy replied, "but something questionable is going on around here." He didn't want to worry Mama, so he said no more about it for several days, but went to tend his traps more often than usual, trying to determine why he had found so many dead elk carcasses with no teeth in their heads.

Daddy visited each of his neighbors and told them what he had been finding. "Those strangers in town have come for a purpose," Daddy said. "I think they have heard about the price other Elk's Lodge is paying for teeth and they are here to get in some fast, easy money; caring not about the destruction they are making. We will not have the largest elk herd in the world if this slaughtering keeps on."

The ranchers promised Daddy they would go with him and they would investigate the carryings on. They got up in arms when they found the elk were being slaughtered by the hundreds, the meat left for the scavengers, and only the two ivory tusks were taken. Even though only the bull elk have teeth of any importance, cows too were being killed for the one or two dollars their teeth would bring.

The ranchers of Flat Creek held a consultation then rode to town in a posse. They told the game warden and sheriff what was happening. "These foreigners have started a killing, now we are going to end one with them if something isn't done right away," one man said.

"I'll tell you what we will have to do," spoke Si Ferrin, the sheriff. "We will appoint deputy sheriffs, and assistant game wardens and lay for these tusk hunters."

The county seat being over two hundred miles away made it almost impossible to make an arrest for game killing as licenses weren't required, and if they made an arrest, it was almost impossible to get a conviction.

A meeting time and place was appointed at Mr. Hanshew's cabin on the Gros Ventre River. Mr. Hanshew was appointed chairman of the committee. During the meeting, Daddy brought up the fact that if they pressed charges against these brazen killers, they may even start a killing among the men of Jackson or harm their families. Each man present, in turn, marched around a table, voiced his opinion then shook Mr. Hanshew's hand, and promised to stand behind him.

His reply was, "Listen you fellers, if any of you here tonight in this room is a scart to take hold of the rope, let him get up and leave now." Not one man proved to be a coward.

That night when Daddy came home, he was whistling, but not very gleefully. He told Mama about the strangers in town and all about the meeting. He said, "We are going to warn them to leave or they will be shot. I have to leave by daylight in the morning to meet many other appointed men and we are going out to do our duty. Do you think you can take care of the chores for a few days if I'm gone that long?" He warned Mama to keep us children in the house and not answer the door to any strangers until he returned.

"Dear, do be careful," Mama said the next morning, as she kissed him good-bye, and buttoned the top button on his sheep-lined overcoat.

"I will dear," he said as he finished buttoning the lower three buttons, "but don't look for me until you see me. This may take several days. These pesky elk have caused us so much grief in the past few years, I almost wish I had never seen one of them, but we have to protect them, even if they are eating us right out of the house and barn."

Daddy kissed Mama on the forehead, strapped his webs to his feet, and departed quietly to meet the other men.

Daylight was barely beginning to break. Mama stood at the window and watched him swing his arms in rhythm with his legs as he webbed away. She glanced up at Old Timer as he left the door, and again as he dropped below a gully. It took him sixteen minutes to disappear out of sight.

The men met at the designated place, and they decided

they should split up in pairs, each pair going in a different direction, then meet back in so many hours, to report the findings. This they did, and every couple found dead carcasses galore with the tusks extracted.

The tusk hunters had been tipped off so they hid in a makeshift cabin in an undiscovered place for days. While there, they planned a scheme which threw the wardens completely. The wardens were hot on their trails one day, when a terrible blizzard covered their tracks, forcing the wardens to return to their cabin. Most of the time it was sub-zero weather, making the investigation even more difficult.

One day, the wardens scattered like bloodhounds. They found tracks galore of men and webs. They knew they were on their trails and would soon find a whole company of them. Then suddenly the tracks ended and only elk tracks could be found. This completely puzzled the wardens. These men's tracks were all leading in one direction, and all ended abruptly.

Finally, Mr. Goe called to Daddy. "Come here, Jim!" Daddy went to him. He was bent down examining a funny thing made of wood. "Look here," he said. "They have made stilts out of wooden blocks, nailed elk feet to the bottom of them and have been using these on their feet, making it appear to be elk tracks all over."

"Well, I'll be—" Daddy said. "Can you beat that? They are making their killing without leaving human tracks." They took these stilts back with them to the meeting that night.

In the meanwhile, another couple of wardens found the makeshift cabin where these man had been hiding. They had it cleverly designed in a clump of willows.

The game wardens decided to call all the ranches to help. About sixty men gathered at Mr. Hanshew's home and they agreed to give these men twenty four hours to leave or they would be killed. The ranchers no longer called themselves "squatters," but "doers of duty."

While this meeting was going on, many of the tusk hunters had hid themselves in the bushes near the house and intended to kill every man as he came out the door of the cabin, but Mr. Hanshew's faithful dog saved them from this destruction. He barked excitedly at the men in the brush, warning the men in the house of the danger.

The men stayed in the house all night and by morning the tusk hunters had gone. It would have been impossible for them to remain outdoors all night without freezing to death. It was a wretched night.

The next morning, the wardens and ranchers tracked the hunters to their cabin. The sheriff, a big, husky man, afraid of no man's bluff, knocked on the door. One man came to the door, opened it and shoved a long rifle in Si's face. Si grabbed the muzzle of the gun in one hand, stroked his muscular neck with the other and spoke in husky words. "Come on out, every one of you, with your hands in the air." Then Si ordered, "Every one of you line up against that wall! And keep your arms in the air! That means you too," he said as he pointed the muzzle of the gun and scrutinized a bewhiskered, droopy-eyed monster which resembled a beast more than a man. If any one of you makes a move, you will either drop dead instantly or die of lead poisoning.

"Now we've had all the killing we are gong to have around here, unless you can't understand, we stand for law and order, but the next blood shed won't be from elk— understand?" Then he shouted all the louder, causing the cords to stand out in his thick neck: "But from human flesh, and you too will be left dead in your tracks for the scavengers to devour. If anyone has anything to say, let him say it now."

Each of the fifty nine men behind Si's back stepped one step closer to Si.

One little mousy looking man stepped out of the line-up

of tusk hunters. He was smaller in stature than the rest, but he seemed to be leader and spokesman and said, in a trembling voice, "We promise to be gone within twenty four hours if our lives may be spared."

The only other word uttered came from Si. "Dismissed!"

Daddy and the rest of the men returned to their homes. Mama was so glad to see Daddy for she felt sure, after the second night, he had been killed.

The next day, the tusk hunters loaded up a large collection of heads, and some horns. One of them went to town to tell the game department and the residents in a local bar that they had killed a game warden up the country. Naturally, everyone rushed there to see about the killing, and while the settlers were in the upper valley, the tusk hunters escaped over the mountain into Idaho and succeeded in shipping the heads and horns to California. In their excitement to get away, they left a galvanized wash basin full of valuable ivory teeth.

The men of the town could see they had been tricked as no warden had been killed, so immediately two of them began following the tusk hunters. They didn't catch up to them until they reached Los Angeles, California, where they found some of the men and their loot. These men were brought back to Wyoming for jeopardy.

The Elk Lodge then discontinued using the teeth in emblem jewelry.

In spite of the slaughtering that took place this winter, the remaining herd returned the next winter to feed from the ranchers' stacks.

The ranchers held another meeting and elected Daddy as scribe to write the Governor of Wyoming a letter to see what could be done to reimburse the ranchers for the loss they took each winter. They received word that something would be done to reimburse them, and a plan was being worked on, whereby the elk would be fed.

From then on, the ranchers on Flat Creek were hired to raise hay to feed the starving elk. And by being hired to feed the starving elk, the ranchers also ate much better.

Chapter XXI
COUNTING ELK

As the time went on, the Federal Government became even more concerned about the elk situation than the State of Wyoming had been. Great herds came down from, not only the mountains close by, but as far as Yellowstone Park. Some of the farmers refused to raise hay to feed them. It became a big job.

Daddy was contacted one day by some Federal Government officials to see if he was willing to sign a contract to feed the elk. His responsibilities would be: figure out how many tons of hay it would take to feed them; see that the feeding grounds as well as the haystacks were fenced with high enough fences that the elk couldn't jump over; keep a count of how many would come to be fed each winter; and, the biggest job of all, keep them fed. The Federal Government wanted every elk rounded up and then brought down from the hills onto the feeding grounds.

Daddy said to one of the officials: "Supply me with one other man, a good saddle horse for him, and I'll take old Doll, and we will get the elk counted in the hills, but I cannot do the job alone. I will not sign any such contract until I know more about it."

After these men returned to Cheyenne, they discussed the situation with State Government officials and decided to appeal the issue to the Isaac Walton League for help. They carefully considered it, and the Isaac Walton League decided the wild game in Wyoming needed help, perhaps even more than any other place, due to the great herds and the extreme severity of the winters.

A man by the name of Dall deWeese was sent in March, from Canon City, Colorado, to be Daddy's companion while counting elk in the hills. They were to take Flat Creek territory and everything north to Grovont country, while

Mr. Elmer Moody and Mr. Felix Buckenroth were selected to go to the Hoback area to count.

Mr. deWeese arrived in town on a Saturday, Daddy there to meet him, with Big Bite and Bally pulling Sleigh-Bob, found him a very kind, old gentleman, in his middle sixties, with a mop of heavy, white, wavy hair. He looked distinguished and well-to-do. He enjoyed his trip home in Sleigh-Bob with the horses. He asked Daddy all the questions he could think of about the territory, how he helped settle it, and how long the elk had been bothering the ranchers.

Slumber Tuff was put back in the kitchen for Mr. deWeese. Mama apologized for the bed as well as for the room. His tone of voice showed pity for us, yet he had gratitude in his heart for all Mama did to make him comfortable.

Mama was a most gracious hostess, even though she had to wash with a washboard in Tiny Tin, Mr. deWeese's clothes were washed along with the rest of ours, his bed changed often, and his feather mattress fluffed daily.

Every night, we children stayed up as late as we were allowed to listen to Mr. deWeese tell stories. He told us all about his family; how his wife died in their early married life, leaving him with three small children. He told how he came into a lot of money; that he had a luxurious home with a nurse to tend his children while they were small, and also had a maid.

One night, as we all sat close to Pot-Belly, he told this story, which was of lasting interest to us.

"My daughter, Blanche, gave me a lot of concern while growing up. Not that she desired any sin in life, but being so ambitious, I couldn't keep her occupied. When she started talking about boys and marriage, I handed her a saw and an ax, and told her to go out into the orchard, cut down the best tree she could find, and bring it to me. I instructed her with a few rules. They were: 'You may start anywhere you want,

177

go down any row you choose, until you get to the end of that row, then you must go to another one, until you find the most perfect tree, but remember you cannot backtrack over any territory you have already covered. Now go with my blessings, and good luck daughter.'

"After being gone about an hour, she returned with a good tree. I looked it over and asked, 'Is this the best tree in the orchard, dear?' I knew there were better.

"She replied, 'No, father, this isn't the best, but you told me not to turn back, so I had to choose this one, because I had nearly come to the end of the trees.'

"Then I told her, 'This is the lesson I want to instill within you, dear. Remember in life as you go out into the world to choose a companion, you can only have one man, so keep your eyes open, and choose the best one possible the first time, because once you choose him, you can't go back over your life and wish you had chosen some other one.' Blanche did a lot of pondering from then on, and chose quite wisely."

Mr. deWeese told us he had been a member of the Isaac Walton League since its organization, and was one of the men present in the meeting when a man was to be chosen to go to the rescue of the elk herds. He volunteered, thinking it would be a rest from the city, his office duties, and was quite sure a change in climate would improve his health. "I always wanted to get out in the country and rough it for comfort," he told us again, as he had told Daddy on their way to Poverty Flats.

"We'll get up in time to let you see dawn break in the morning," Daddy said. "And you can see the sun coming up over Whistler's Peak, cold, crisp, and clear, then you'll be sure to agree there is something special about this country."

The first day out in the hills, Mr. deWeese suffered intensely. The snow was up to the horses' knees in places. All of his one hundred seventy pounds of flesh and bones

178

rocked and rolled in the saddle, bundled in a heavy parka, big mittens, woolen socks, and overshoes. He was so stiff when they returned home that night, he couldn't sit down to eat his supper. Sun and windburned, his face glistened like a red-hot coal and showed definite marks where the parka hadn't covered. Yes, this day had made a profound impression upon him.

The next day, Mr. deWeese felt ill. He got out of bed, but couldn't walk. Daddy gave him some salve to use on his saddle sores. The same salve used for cows sore udders, on us children if we got a burn, and on our lips for cold sores, surely it would be good for saddle burns too. Daddy told him if he could manage to climb into the saddle, the second day was always easier than the first and he would limber right up.

Mr deWeese didn't want to appear soft from city life, nor did he want sympathy. He ate breakfast standing up. When he straddled his horse again, he said, "I'm sure this horse spread at least two feet wider during the night."

"We'll take it slow and easy, and will only take in one draw today," Daddy promised. "After all, we have a month to do this job before these elk will be leaving the lowlands and migrating back to the high hills for a safer place to rear their young. No need covering a lot of territory for the first few days."

"Are the young always born in the spring of the year, Jim?" asked Mr. deWeese.

"Yep! You see, the mating takes place in the autumn, about the first of September 'till mid-October. It is called the rutting season. This is an interesting time to be in the hills. You can hear the bugling calls across the canyons. It sounds much like a high pitched aaaaaa-eeeeee-eough whistle, or a noise from a bugle. This is called 'the challenge call,' even though they don't always do it to challenge, but more for a partial outlet for their pent-up desires, but then

179

the bulls commence to fight for mastery of their harems."

"How many cows usually follow a bull, Jim?"

"Anywhere from about ten to as many as sixty."

"Really! How old are cows before they give birth to calves?"

"Most usually two years old," Daddy answered.

"Have you ever witnessed a fight between bull elk?"

"Yes, several times, in the early fall the neck of a bull elk commences to swell. Sometimes it swells so large it even bulges his eyes. You know then the mating season is on, and the meat isn't good to eat. I have seen bull elk kill each other, however, this doesn't often happen, because usually the small bull or the weaker of the two backs off and runs away, then the larger bull goes after another smaller bull he can whip. If he is victorious, he takes his harem and they go off to themselves and start to migrate to grassier, greener meadows."

"I'll tell you something else about elk, Dall, it's what they do if they eat Larkspur."

"Wait a minute, Jim, what is Larkspur?"

"It's a weed which grows about six to eight inches tall with a purple bloom on it. If a domestic cow gets it, it poisons her, and she will lie down and die, but if an elk gets it, it makes him sick and he starts to whirl. He whirls so fast you can't tell his head from his tail. This makes him sick and he regurgitates, then goes right on eating."

"They are a pretty smart animal, aren't they, Jim? Do these bull's horns grow larger each year, and is that the way you tell the age of the animal?."

"Yes, you are partly right," said Daddy, "but by mid-March each year, they commence to drop their antlers then they look much like the female, except for their larger size. Each year, the bull grows a complete new set of antlers, but usually larger than his last year's set. The prongs or tines of these antlers have names. The first prong is called a brow,

180

the second prong is bez, the third trez, the fourth royal, the fifth, sixth, seventh, and eighth are called crown. While you are here, I would like to show you some horns in people's homes. Some are used for hat racks, some are made into chairs, some decorate flower gardens. They are even used as door and knife handles. They're soft enough to carve and easy to whittle. Some very large heads have a spread of antlers sixty to sixty five inches wide. The average mature bull has six long points on each antler, although seven and eight points aren't uncommon," explained Daddy.

"How much would a big bull elk weigh, Jim?"

"Anywhere from seven hundred to one thousand pounds."

Then Mr. deWeese said, "Jim, I think I weigh about that much now. Perhaps I could make it better on foot. I think I'll walk and lead my horse." He stood up in the stirrups, tried to lift one leg over the saddle, but it wouldn't come. He tried the other leg and found it as useless. He managed to push his body over the saddle seat and slide off backwards over the horse's rump, sinking nearly to his knees in the snow. He tried pulling his legs out of the snow, but they wouldn't move. Daddy leaned on his saddle horn and began to worry. They were several miles from home, and he didn't know how to get Mr. deWeese back astraddle the horse. He turned the horses around and coaxed Mr. deWeese back to the saddle. Mr deWeese climbed back with Daddy's assistance, but turned so as to ride side saddle all the way back, and once remarked, "I could surely enjoy the cushions and comforts of home."

They only counted six elk standing on a windswept knoll that day.

When Mr. deWeese finished his supper, he said, "I think I shall turn in early tonight." He took his pillow in both hands, shuffled, pounded, and made a dent in it. We heard him heave a sigh, then yawn and say to himself, "One more day nearer the end."

Daddy decided it best to lay off the next day so they went to town in Sleigh-Bob with Big Bite and Bally. The spring seat wasn't quite as bad as a saddle, but Mr. deWeese thought he had seen better days, and ways to spend them.

We had one of the thrills of our lives that night, when the two men returned home. Mr. deWeese had bought us a case of oranges and a bushel of apples—a real luxury in our lives. He called us outside that night and gave us a lecture about the stars. He told us that in many cities he had visited, the stars were never seen, because the bright lights of the city outglistened them each night. He taught us to appreciate stars, their light and glory.

After we were tucked into bed that night, we heard Daddy say, "Getting the elk herds out of these mountains down to the feeding grounds will be a much greater task than I thought, Dall. I can't understand elk. They are as stubborn as humans when you try to work with them. You can't drive them down, nor can you drive them back."

While counting, they found many diseased and scabby looking elk and they shared the conviction that this condition was caused by starvation.

"I'll tell you, Dall, the winter of 1911 was the hardest winter on the elk. They starved to death by the hundreds. That winter, it rained hard for several days, then it froze, then it snowed on top of the ice, and the elk couldn't paw for food. I actually saw dead elk so thick that you cold walk on dead carcasses for miles. They would get to the haystacks, but were so weak they couldn't get over the fences to the hay."

"Now, here we are at the Roy McBride place. He and his wife, Maggie, lived in this little dirt roofed house, and they had a small herd of cattle, and one day Roy was going to the field to check his cattle, and here came a pack of wolves after them.

182

Roy was stunned, only for a moment, and he ran to the house and got his long-barreled rifle. He shot over their heads, and between them and the cattle. This confused the wolves and they turned toward Roy, and he picked them off one at a time, and got the whole pack. He skinned them out and put their hides on boards to dry. Hides like those were quite valuable at that time."

Roy McBride and the pack of wolves

"Do you remember how many wolves were in the pack, Jim?"

"Yes, Roy gave me a copy of the picture. There were six."

It wasn't hard to get the elk to bunch up in herds. That was their nature. The real trouble came when Daddy and Mr. deWeese tried to get around a herd and count them in a bunch. Often they became frightened and scattered. They could travel many times faster than horses. Sometimes, great herds completely escaped by circling and traveling up the canyons, over ridges and out of sight. When this happened, they would simply estimate the number of the herd as best they could and add it to the total already counted.

On March tenth, Mr deWeese and Daddy left home, with Black Mare, and old Doll, a bed roll, and some food supplies and headed up for Goosewing Ranger Station, stopping the first night at the McCormack ranch at eight o'clock. The next day they reached their destination.

By this time, Mr. deWeese, completely used to the saddle, enjoyed each day. Returning home on the twenty third of March, Daddy had kept a complete record of each day's count and reported 3,339 cows and calves and 501 bulls. Mr. Moody and Mr. Buckenroth counted a total of 9,973 in the Hoback area. They couldn't keep a separate count.

Dead elk

Mr. deWeese had become so adapted to our country ways and felt so welcome and comfortable in our little home, that he lamented the fact he had to return to city life again. We hated to see him go, knowing the rest of the spring months would be lonely ones for us.

The next winter, when the elk came to the feed grounds, Daddy and Troy Pratt were hired to feed them. Daddy fed the upper fields and Troy the lower ones. This proved to be one of our better years. Daddy had a steady income now. We children rode on the feed rack nearly every day, and got to drive the horses while Daddy threw the hay off with a pitchfork. We had so much fun watching the herd come to meet the feed rack every morning, which traveled in a big wide circle. Each elk selected a forkful and stopped to feed from his own little bunch of hay.

The following summer, the Isaac Walton League started buying land from the ranchers on Flat Creek. Some sold for the first price offered them, some held back for a better price, while a few demanded even more.

Almer Nelson was hired to be in charge of this new National Elk Refuge with headquarters about two miles northeast of Jackson. Daddy worked closely and cooperatively with Mr. Nelson, both in getting the elk to the feed grounds, and in feeding them.

These men found the work of the Refuge varied little from any private hay ranch, inasmuch as the land had to be cultivated, irrigated, and the hay harvested. They also found if the winters were hard, each animal consumed from seven and one half pounds of hay per day to ten pounds. They didn't require more because of their slow digestive system, but even this amount made men realize all the more how much hay the elk had been eating, and depriving them of the many years previous to this.

Mama had grown to love "Poverty Flats" dearly by now. She discovered with the setting of each sun, she had passed another day of educational experience. Daddy wasn't anxious to sell, so held off to the bitter end for the highest price possible. There were only three Lumbeck children, Lola, Joe and Dee, the Chambers children and Martha Petersen left to attend Flat Creek School, with Miss Fay Gregory the teacher.

"Sir Hon," Mama said one day, "I can't give up this home. Every one of our children, with the exception of Bertha, has been born here. I have so many fond memories I can't leave."

Daddy knew he had no choice. All the neighbors around him had sold and this land was becoming a rendezvous for game, and would soon be a National Elk Refuge.

As each man sold, he and his family were forced to move off the property within a few weeks. His home was then burned, so all the land could be cleared and planted as soon as possible.

Our front yard served as a grandstand as we stood there one night watching three homes burn. One was the Goes', one the McInellys' and one the Kellys'. Flames reached to the sky, and over the fire, which blazed in the night wind. The heavens all around were red like blood. Tears rolled down the cheeks of both Mama and Daddy.

"A man's hard-earned home going up in smoke like this is more than I can bear," said Daddy. "Each of these places had been built by a conscientious man, who, in most cases, dragged himself part way across the continent to build a home, establish a new life, rub shoulders with honest men, and leave marks so that others may know he and his family passed this way. We will only be remembered as 'Old Warriors' and never get the recognition our pioneer achievements so richly deserve. All this land now," he said, as he swung an outstretched arm to point in all directions, "will become a monument to the elk. No, I shall not sell this home unless they promise me they will never burn nor tear it down."

The next month or two, more homes were burned. We had no close neighbors now. But the saddest of all was the day our schoolhouse went. All the remaining folks on Flat Creek gathered there to get a souvenir. Everyone wanted the little brass bell which was rung by the teacher mornings, noons, and recesses, to call us in. Some got maps from the wall, one got the globe, one got the bucket and blue granite dipper we each had drunk from, however, the desks were taken to the town school as it was in the same district. Seeing the building gutted, one lady remarked, "With this little schoolhouse gone, education just can't go on."

I stood in the doorway and wept bitterly. Mama took me by the hand and led me away as a man threw a bucket of kerosene upon the floor. Cries came from the students and parents. The match wasn't lit until everyone was out of sight, with only one man left to set the torch. After I left the door, I never looked back.

We were the last to sell in the spring of the year. The name of our home would no longer be "Poverty Flats" nor Flat Creek territory, but from now on would be the Wildlife Refuge. Mr. Clifford Hallowell closed the deal with Daddy and promised us our home would never burn, but would stand as a landmark to a great community.

Mr. Dall de Weese

Elk Herd

K.F. Roahen, Billings, Montana
U.S. Fish and Wildlife Service

Chapter XXII
WAGON TRACKS

We remained on the ranch until fall. Daddy was hired to help burn all the remaining homes. Every outbuilding and fence went. Daddy felt remorseful. Every night, he sat for hours in his favorite rocking chair, bent over, holding his head in his hands, rocking back and forth.

Mama tried to cheerfully plan aloud what we could do when we moved to town. "Just think," she said, "we can have electricity, running water, a big bathtub and so many wonderful conveniences."

"What is convenience, Mama?," asked Archie.

"That means we will have some freedom from discomfort, honey," she replied, as she stroked his beautiful head of wavy hair.

We girls hoped for a house big enough that we could have a bedroom for "just girls."

Daddy refused to join in our conversations. This was his home, his land, his life. A place in town would just be a house, a place to eat, and sleep.

He had sold old Doll to John Infinger to use for food for his martin. She became so old, Daddy had said on the first cold night in the fall, for the past three years, "Well, I doubt if old Doll and my mother pull through this winter. They each have rheumatism so bad they can hardly get up."

Mama and my two sisters cried the day the butcher came for the chickens, pigs, and Curley, but Mama didn't let Daddy see her cry. When she saw the butcher coming, she called us children in the house and closed the doors to spare us the injustice which was about to take place. Every living creature on the ranch seemed to know the end had come. Chickens squawked as they were put in wire pens, pigs squealed, and Curley lowed when they tied her down on a flat wagon bed. I couldn't believe any living person could

188

be more criminal-like than is a butcher. The sad part to me was that he climbed on his wagon and went down the road whistling a happy tune. He seemed happy. He had a lot of work to do. For some reason, I couldn't cry. I felt too revengeful.

Mama carefully packed our personal belongings. Everything went. Not one thing did she throw away, burn, or destroy. Daddy tried to coax her into getting rid of all the unnecessary things, but Mama said she didn't have any excess. It had taken everything she had to keep house, and how could she put these things in a much larger house and stretch them out enough to make it look furnished?

Daddy made several trips to town with Lumber Wagon, Big Bite and Bally. The bedding, curtains, pictures and Old Timer were left for the final load.

I wanted to be by myself to have my cry. I went to my castle alone, to recapture memories and visions of some particularly happy moments in my childhood. I looked all around me. Not a bird in the sky, nor any animal of any kind could I see. All was so quiet it was like a tomb. I wept bitterly, yet softly. I didn't want to break the silence of this last memory. I walked, head bowed, back to the empty house, where if anyone spoke, his voice echoed against the barren walls. The door was closed between the bedroom and the kitchen. I opened it to take one last look at the bedroom. There I saw Mama kneeling alone, offering a prayer. I carefully closed the door again and stood in the center of the kitchen floor.

"Where did Mama go?," Daddy asked.

"She'll be here in a minute," I replied.

As she came out, I saw the tears in her eyes, even though she announced radiantly, "All aboard kids, climb on Lumber Wagon—we are ready for our new adventure."

As we started to leave the house, Daddy felt a few rain drops. "Oh, oh," he said, "it is going to rain. Stay in the house a few moments until we see if this cloud is going to pass over or stay." In a few seconds, it was raining hard. Daddy and Mama ran to Lumber Wagon and brought the bedding and all the rest of the things back in the house.

We sat on the bedding in the middle of the kitchen floor for an hour while torrents of rain poured. "We will have to go," Mama said. "There isn't a thing left to eat."

When little Clifford heard this, he started crying, "I'm hungry."

The storm passed over. It traveled east up Flat Creek Canyon.

"Come! Let's go before another storm comes," Daddy said. "It will be dark now before we get there."

We were on our way. We called to Fritz Yellowhair to follow, but he had never been off the ranch since the day he came to live with us. He could not be coaxed to follow. Daddy stopped Big Bite and Bally and said, "Here Berla, hold the lines. I'll have to tie him to the wagon. I left a short rope hanging in the barn, but it will do." Daddy slipped one end of it around Fritz Yellowhair's neck and tied the other end underneath Lumber Wagon. As the wagon started rolling, Fritz still protested. He dug his feet into the earth, trying to hold back. I looked behind us. It had rained so hard the wagon wheels were making deep scars in the earth we all loved so much.

Fritz turned his nose to the sky and howled. A coyote answered his call from the draw. "Could that be Scar-Face, Daddy?," I asked.

"I hardly think so, dear," Daddy said, "but it may be his grandson."

— The End —

190